THIS BOOK BELONGS TO:

••• ••• ••• ••• ••• ••• ••• ••• ••• •••

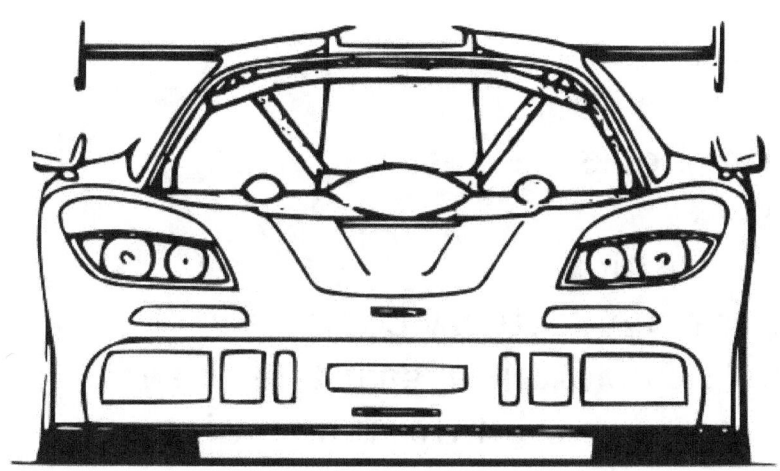

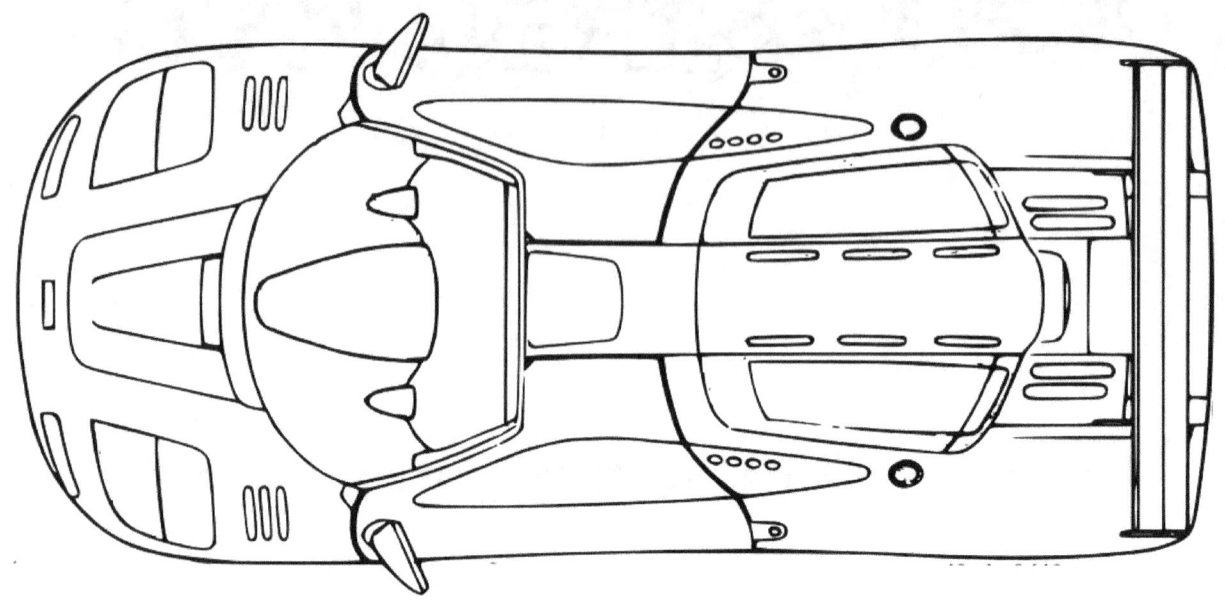

Sports Cars Coloring Book
Muscle Cars Coloring Book
Little Big Coloring Books
Nygaard Books
Playful House Publishing
With illustrations from Vecteezy.com
Copyright © 2024 by Morten Nygaard Pedersen
All rights reserved. No part of this publication may be reproduced, distributed, or transmitted in any form or by any means, including photocopying, recording, or other electronic or mechanical methods, without the prior written permission of the publisher, except in the case of brief quotations embodied in critical reviews and certain other noncommercial uses permitted by copyright law. For information, address playfulhousepublishing@gmail.com
www.playfulhousepublishing.com

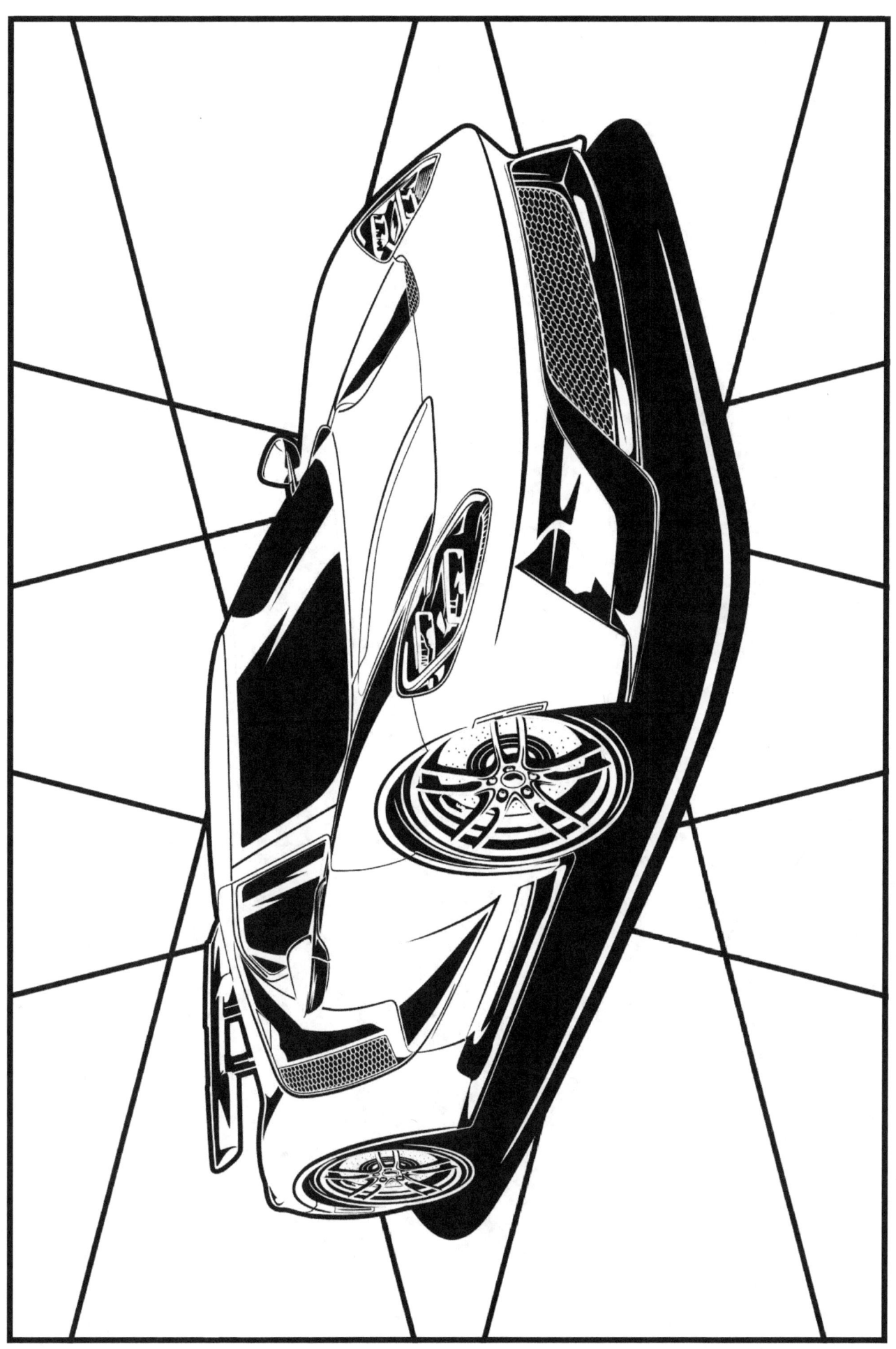

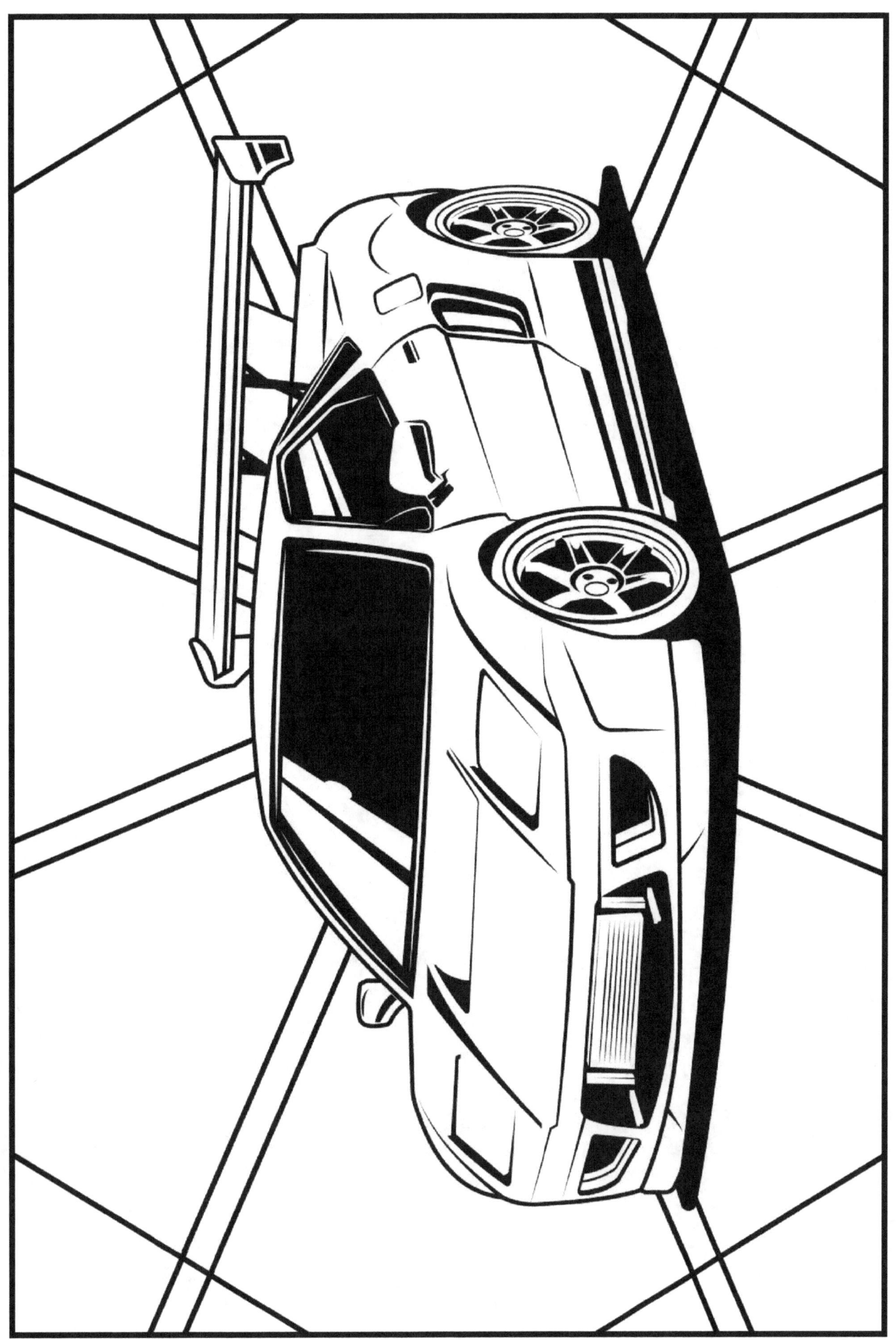

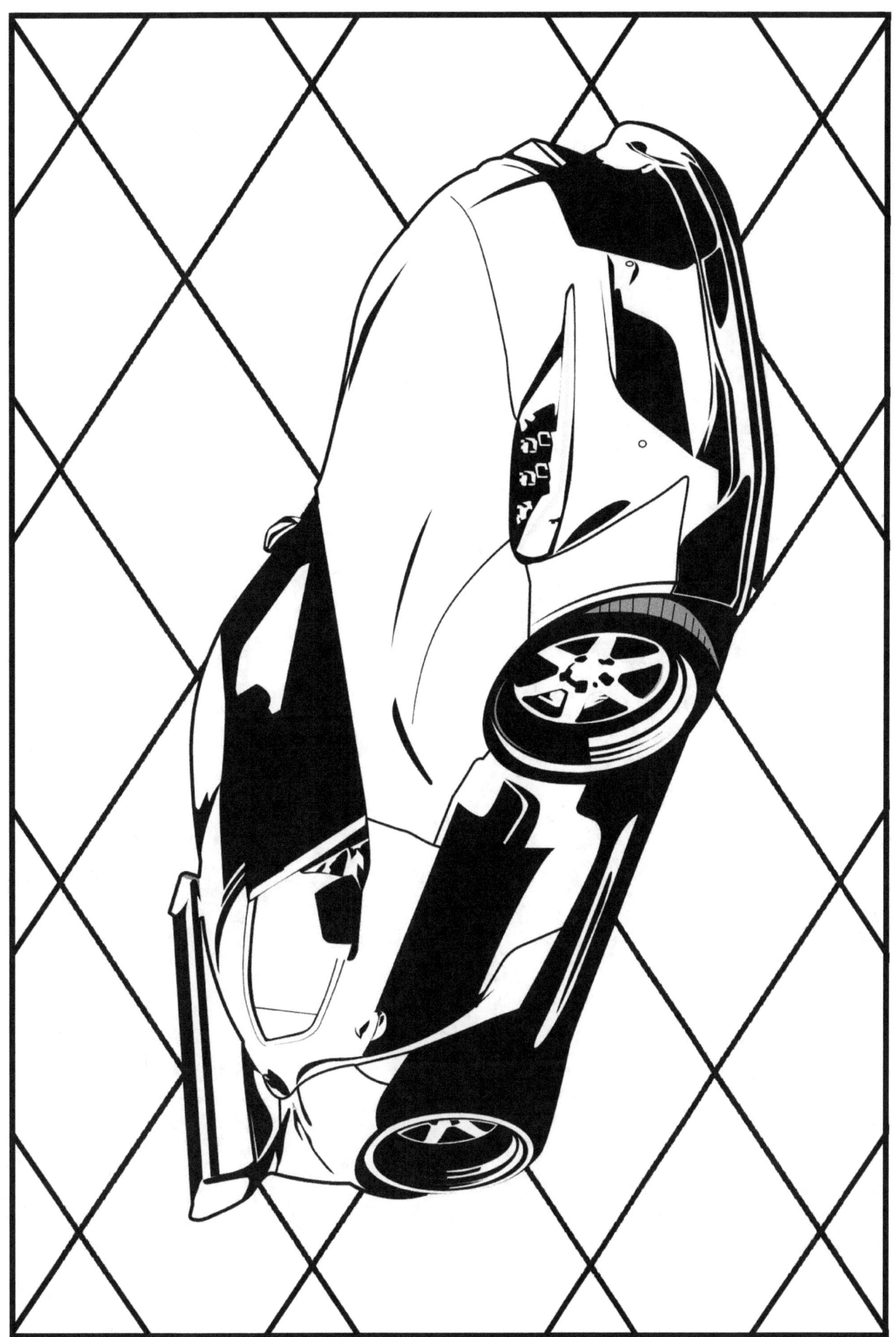

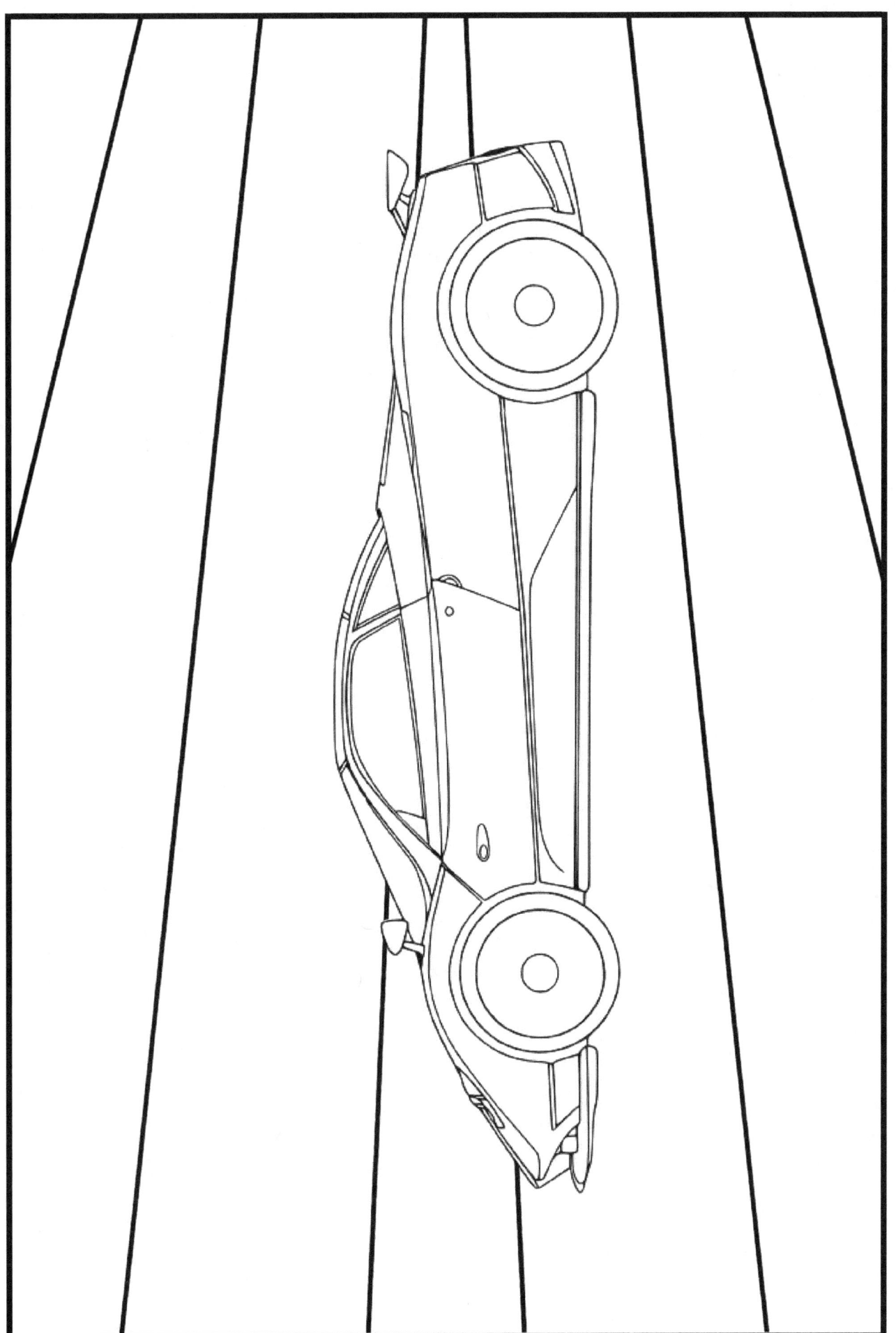

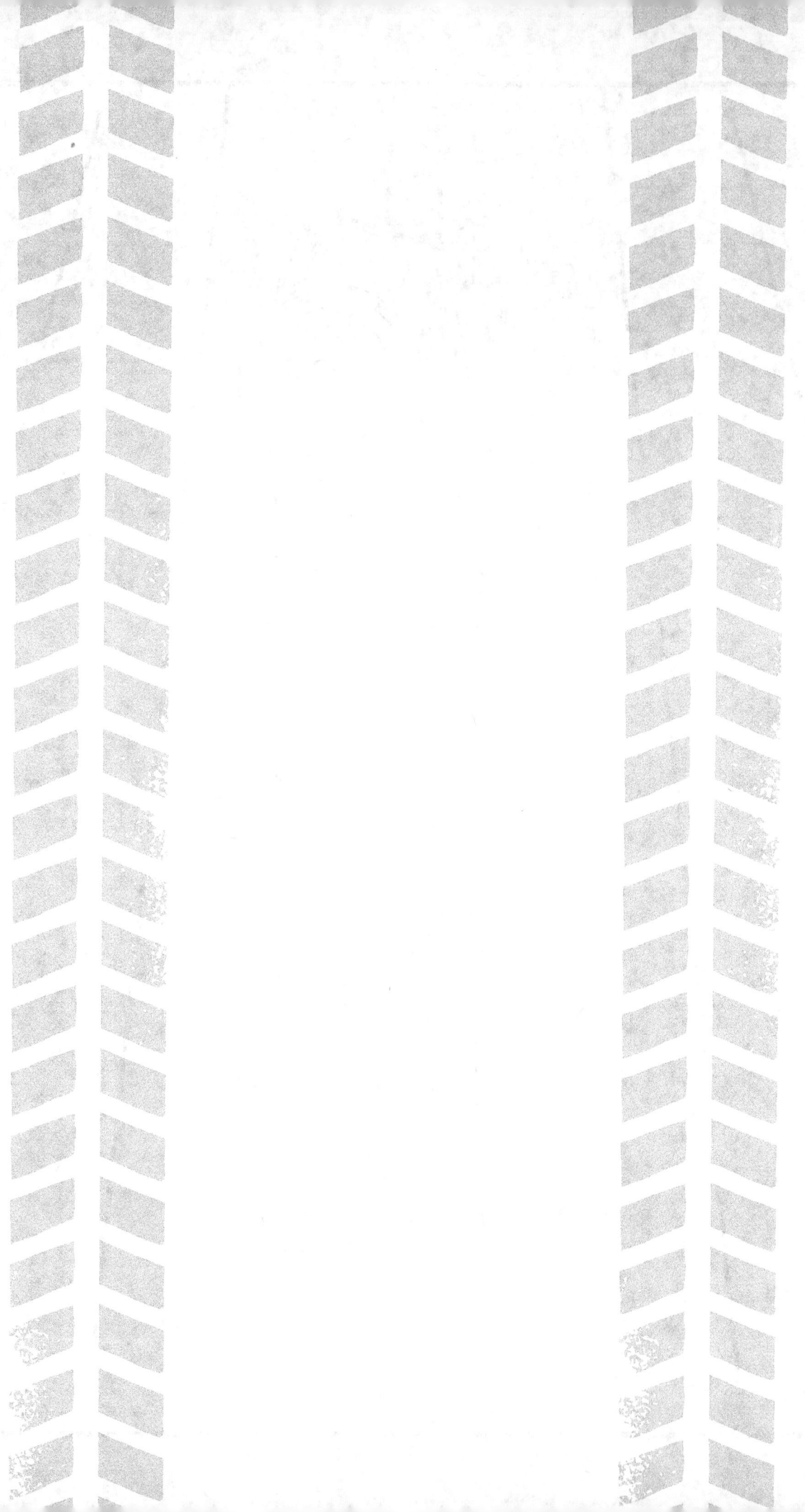

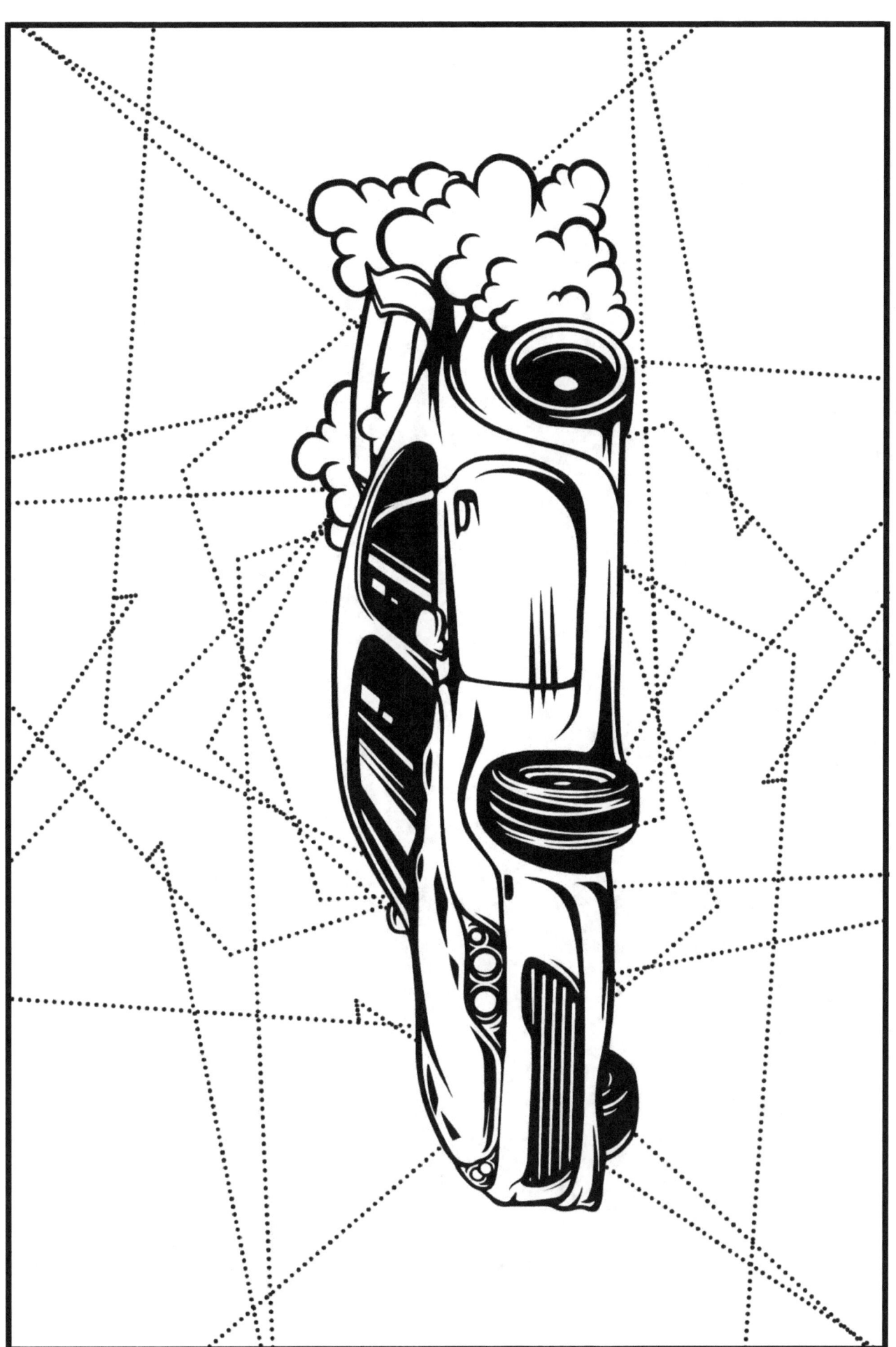

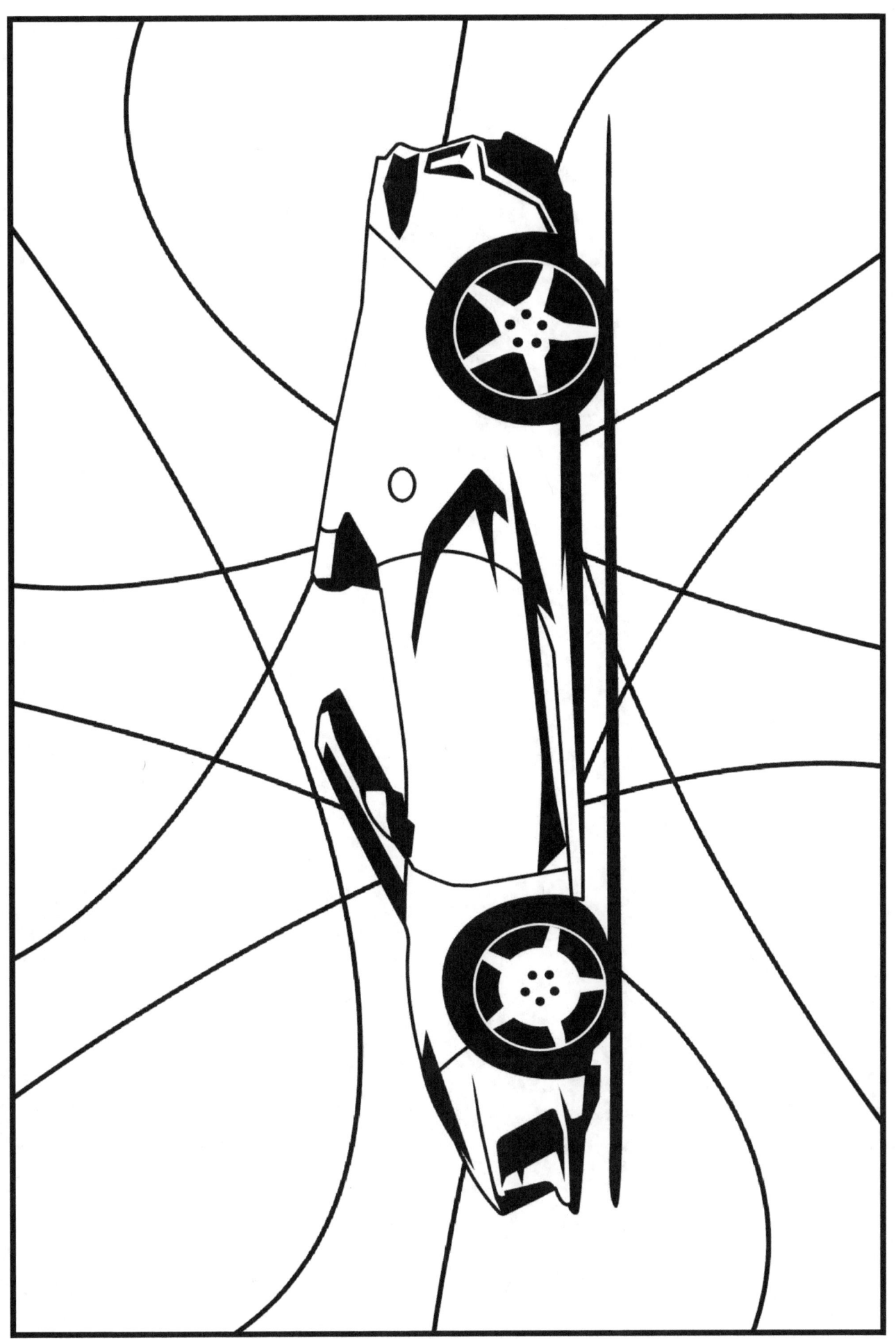

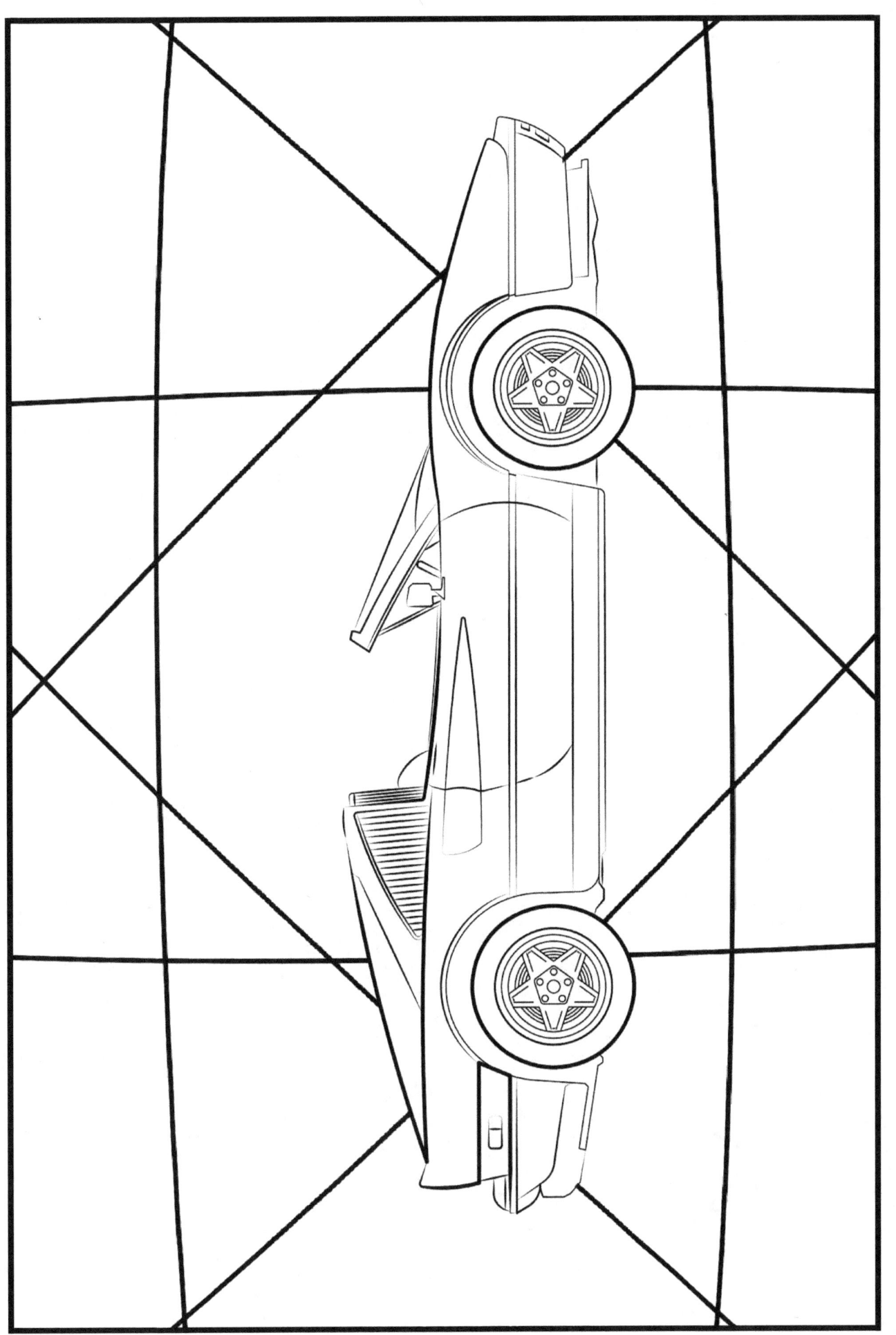

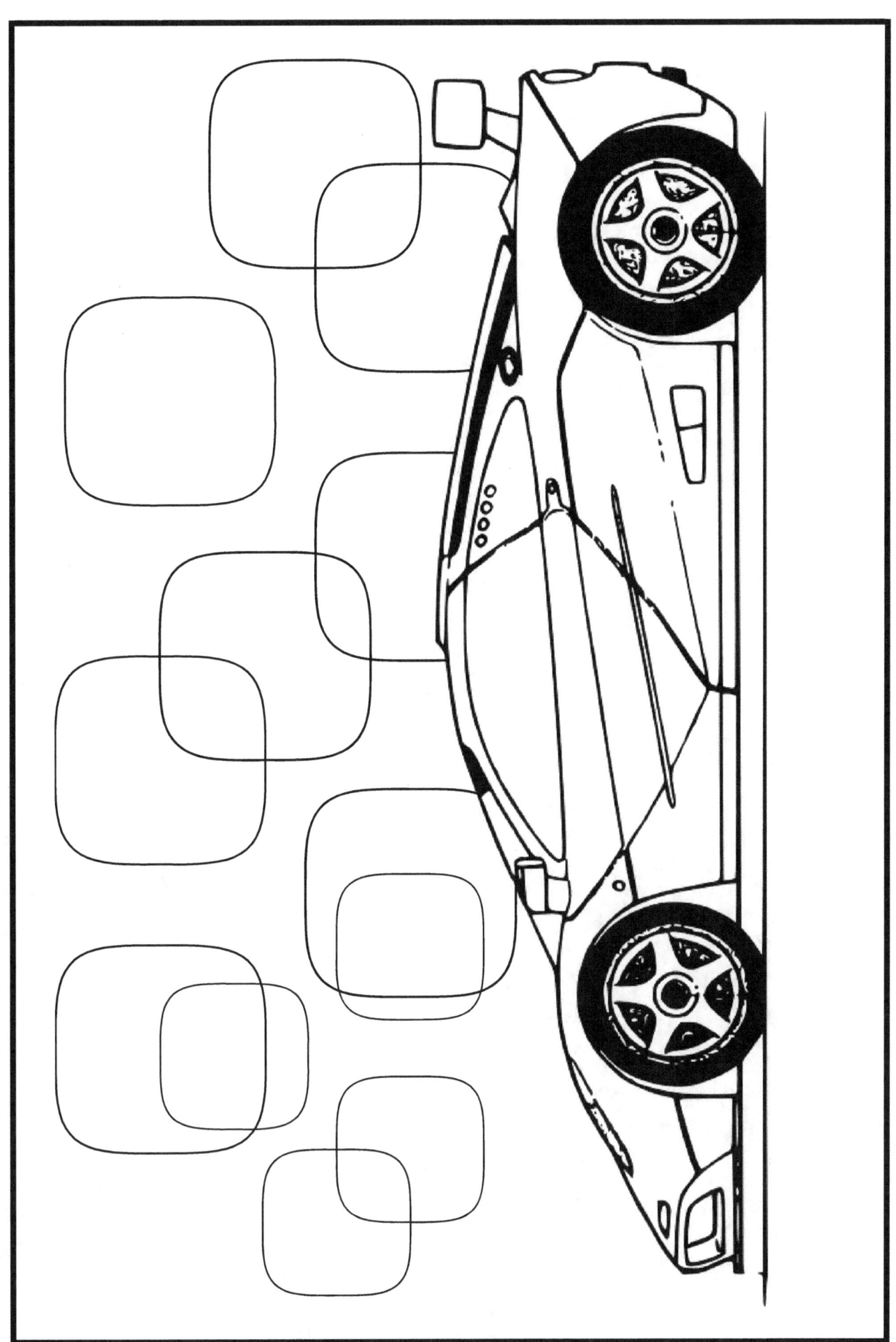

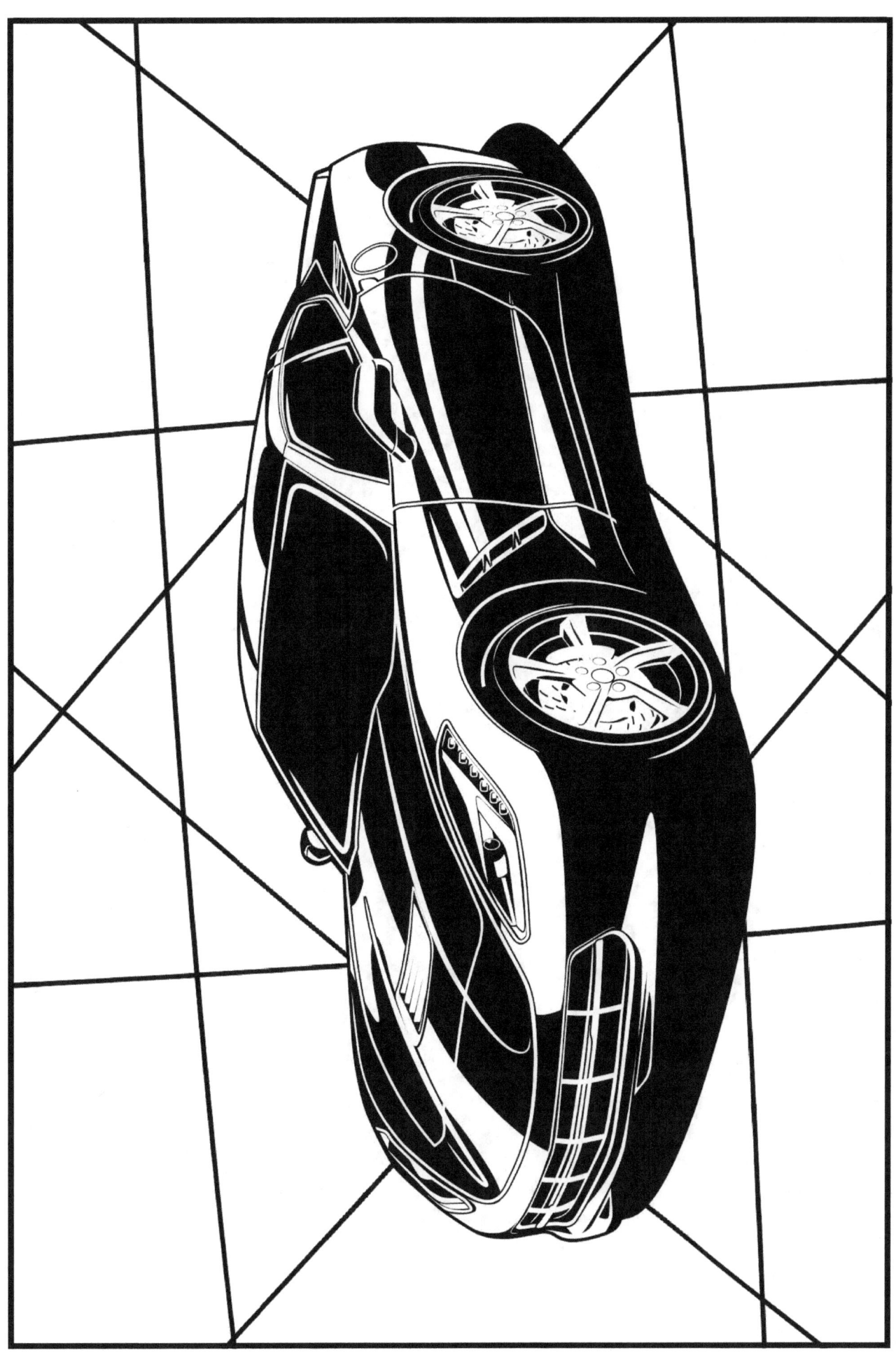

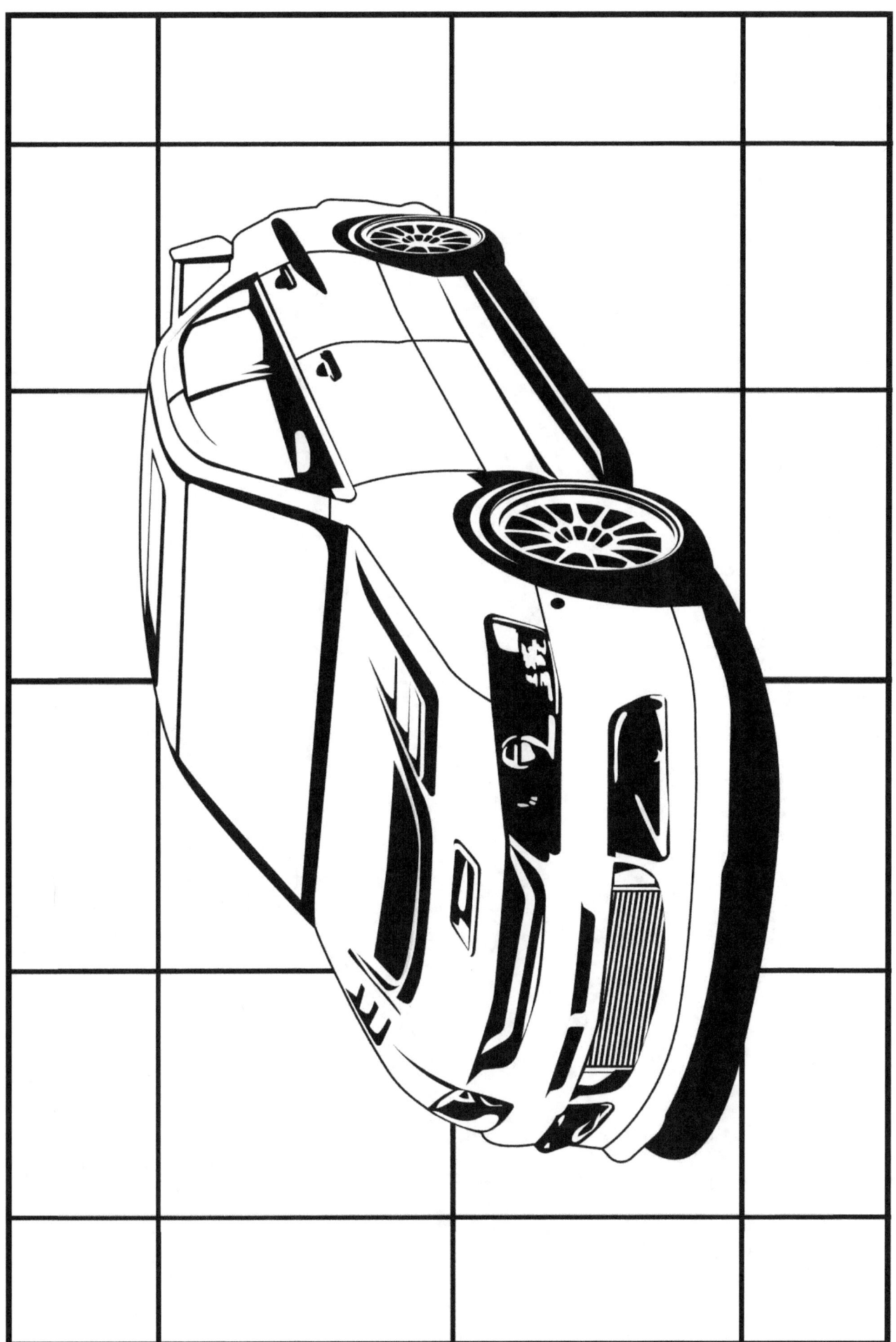

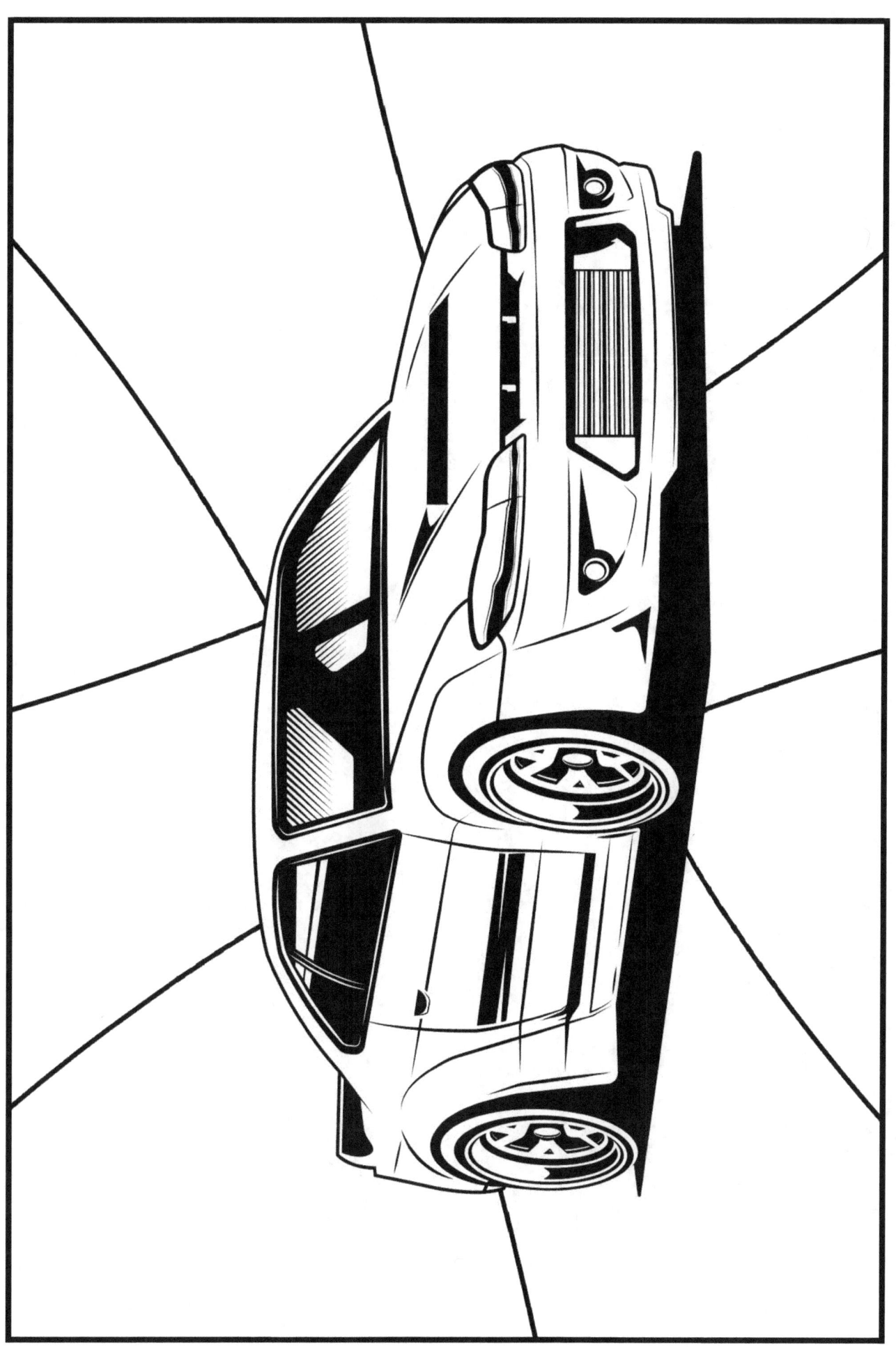

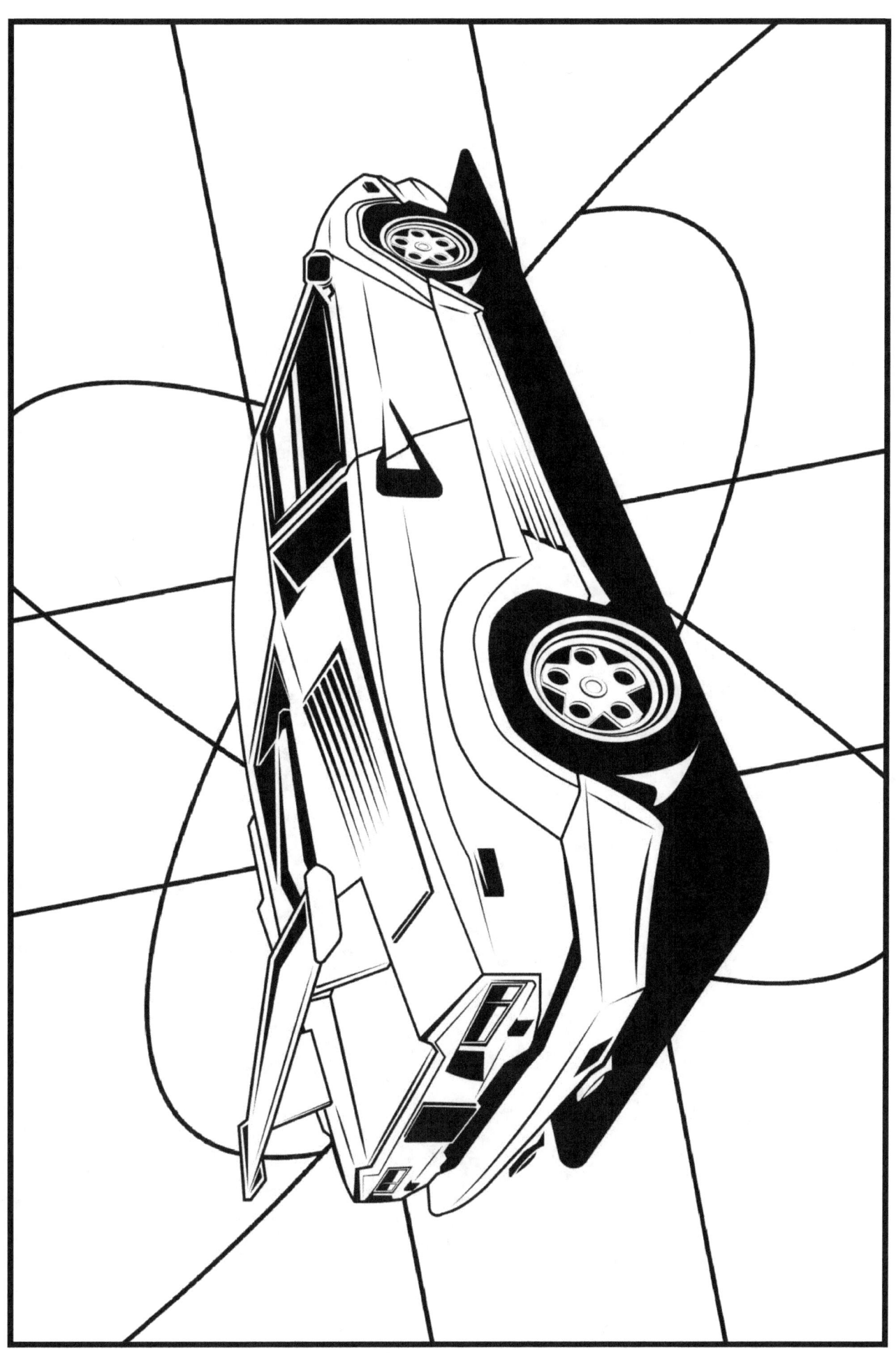

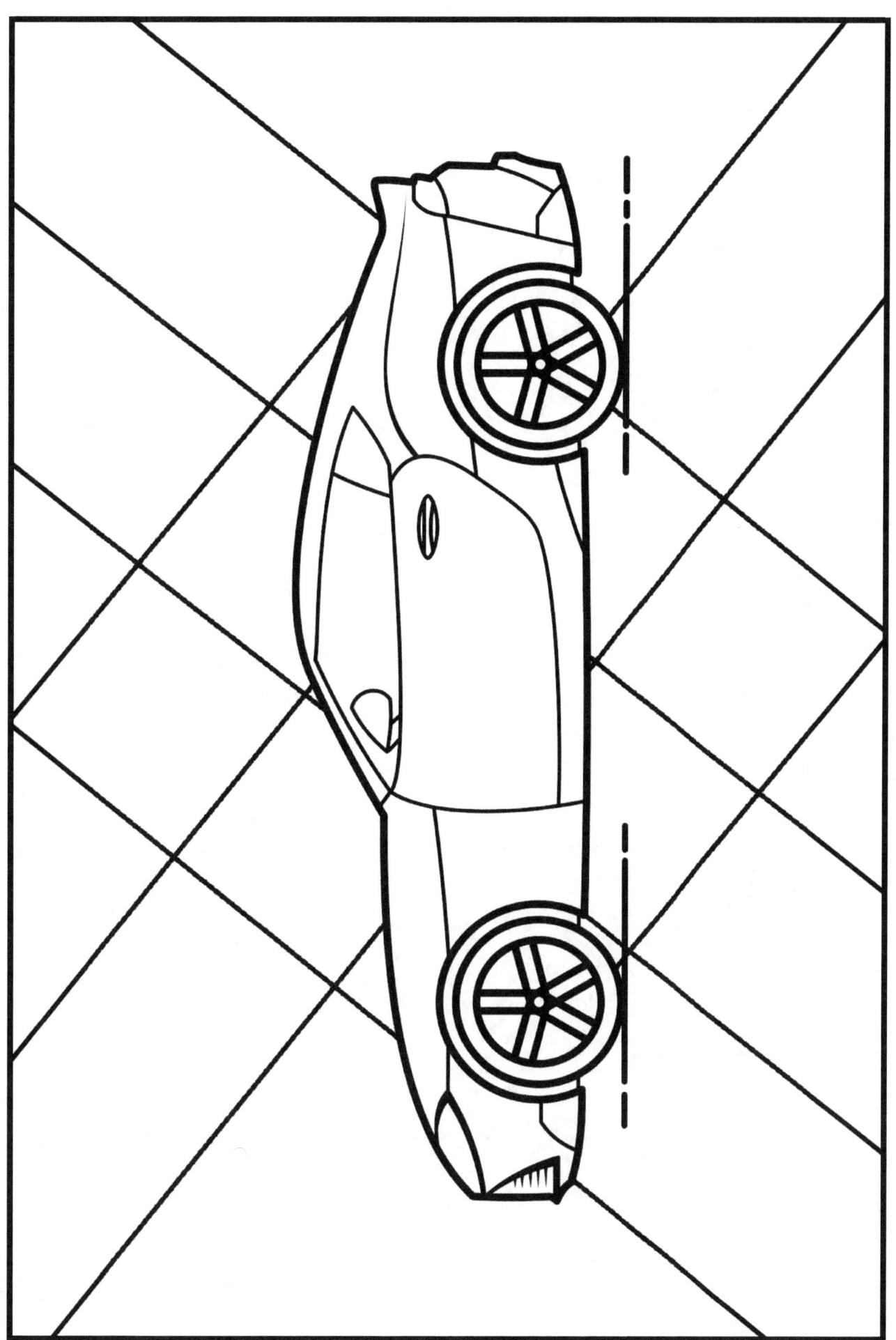

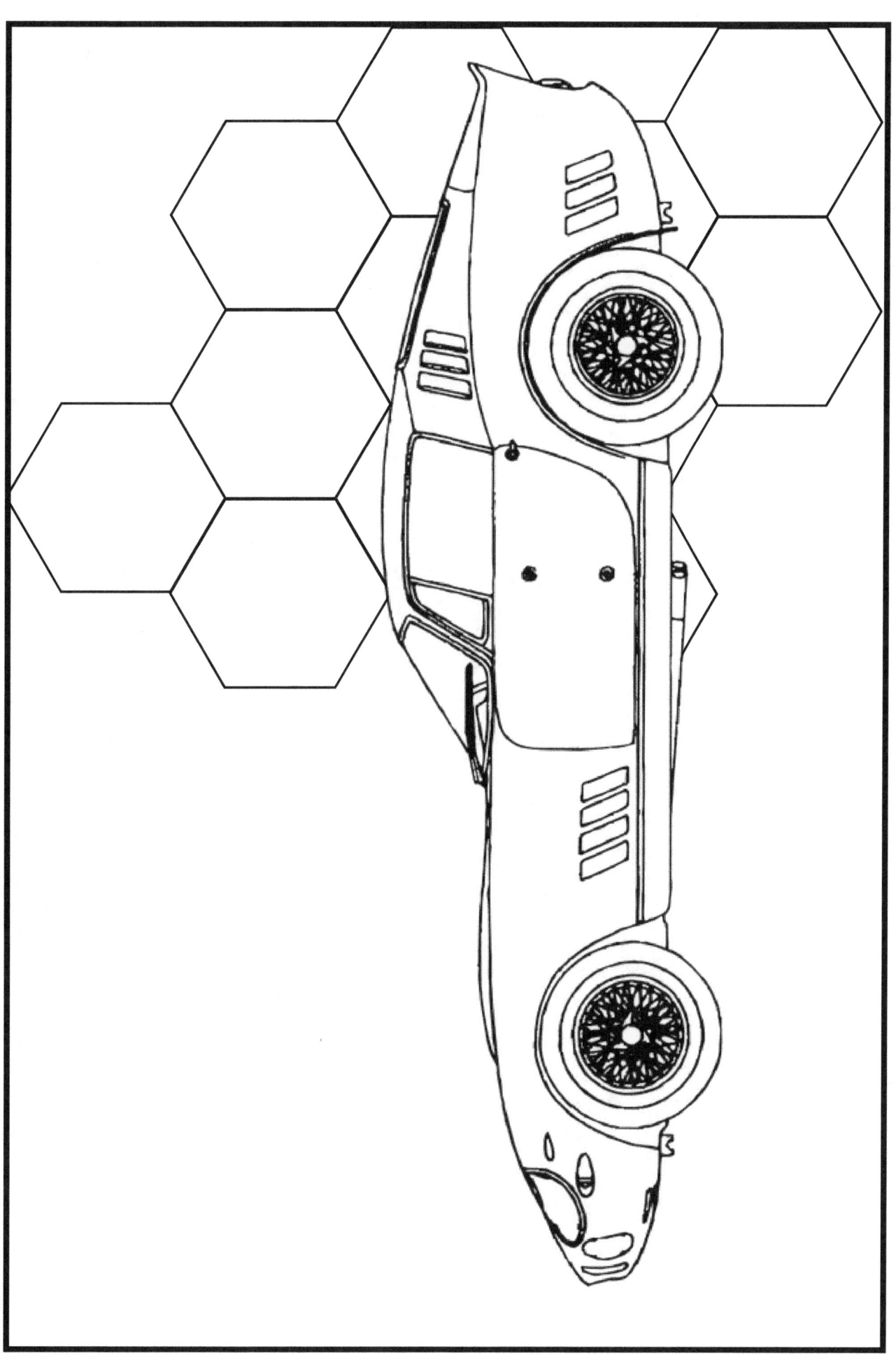

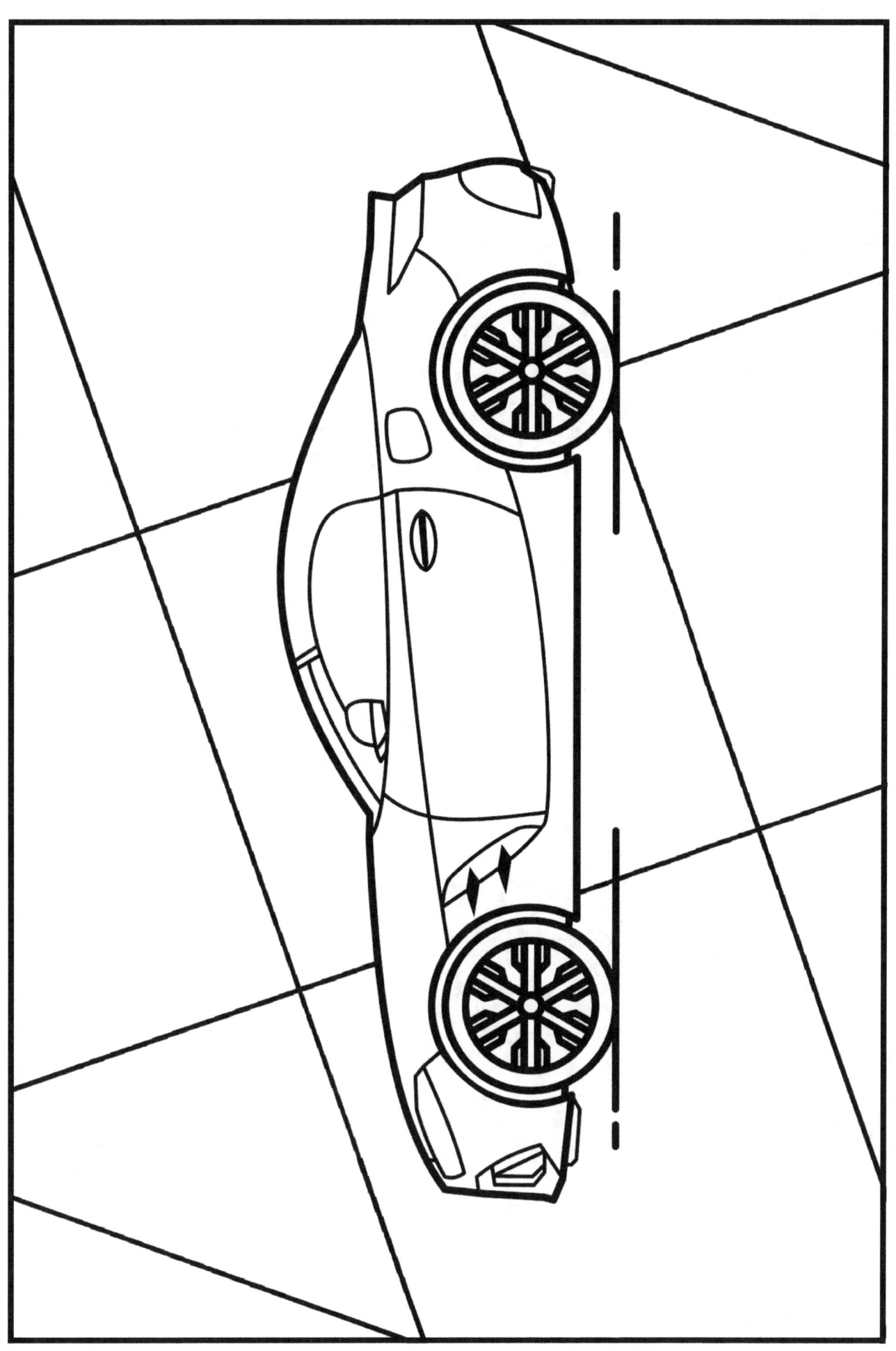

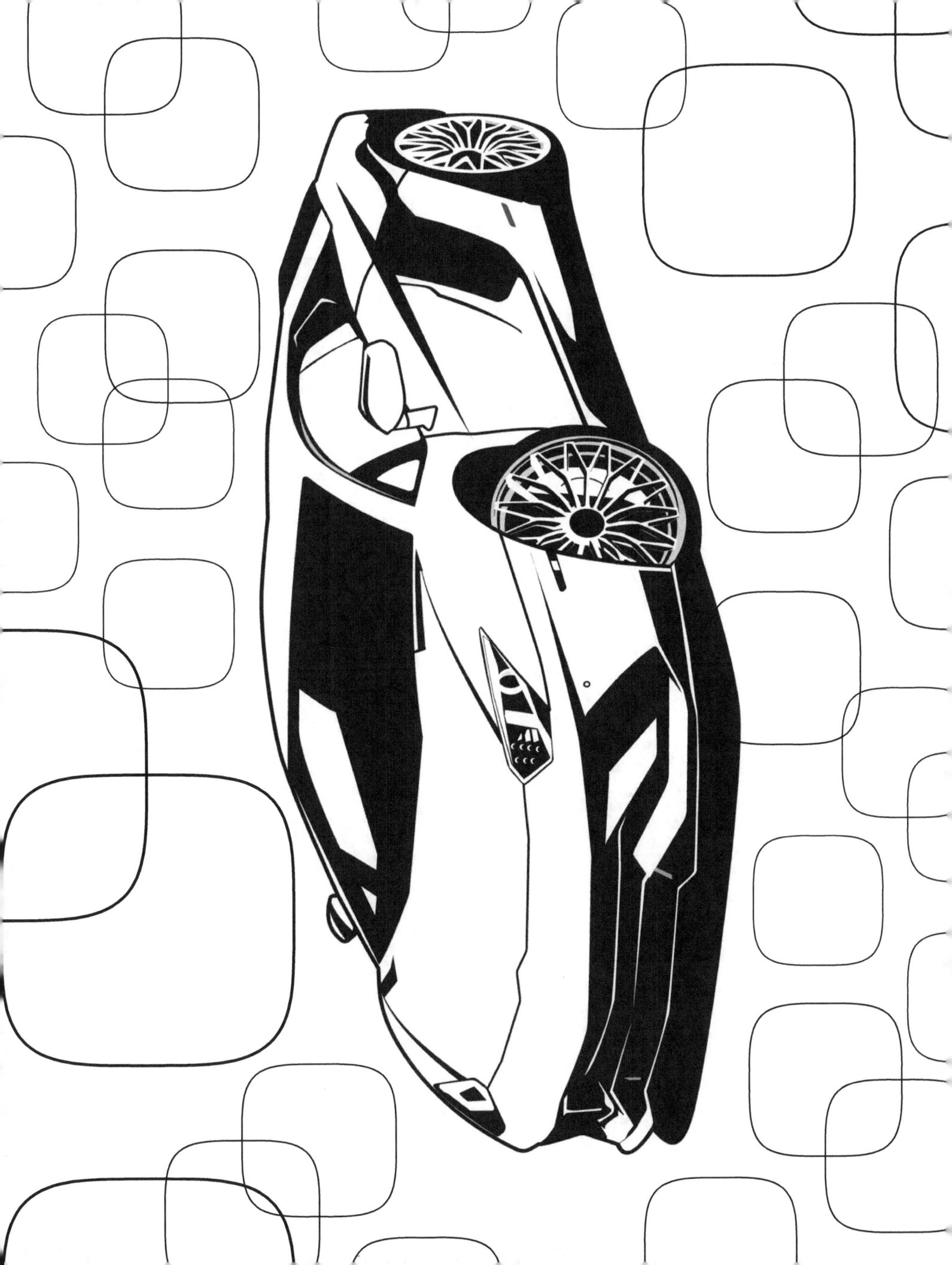

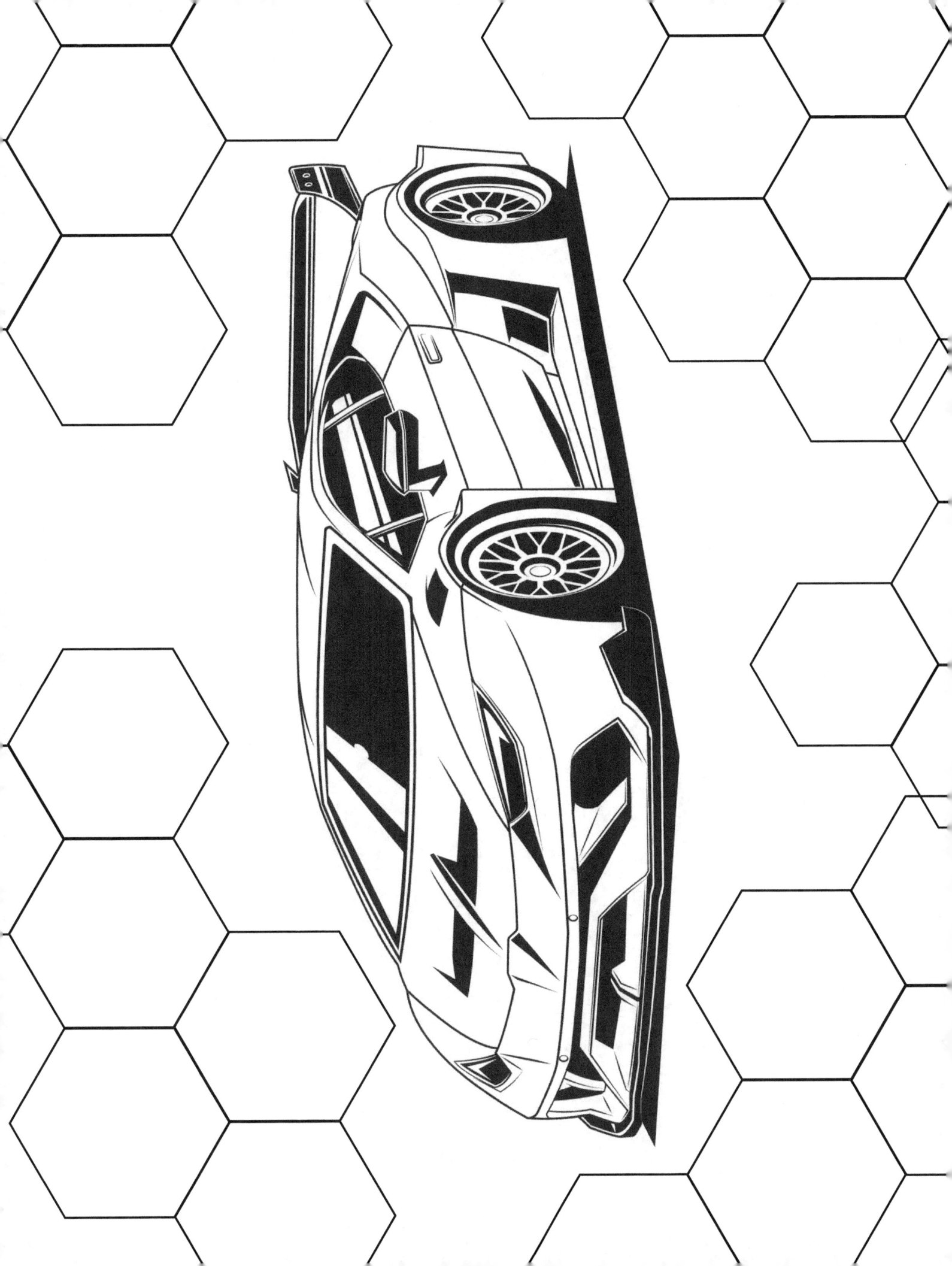

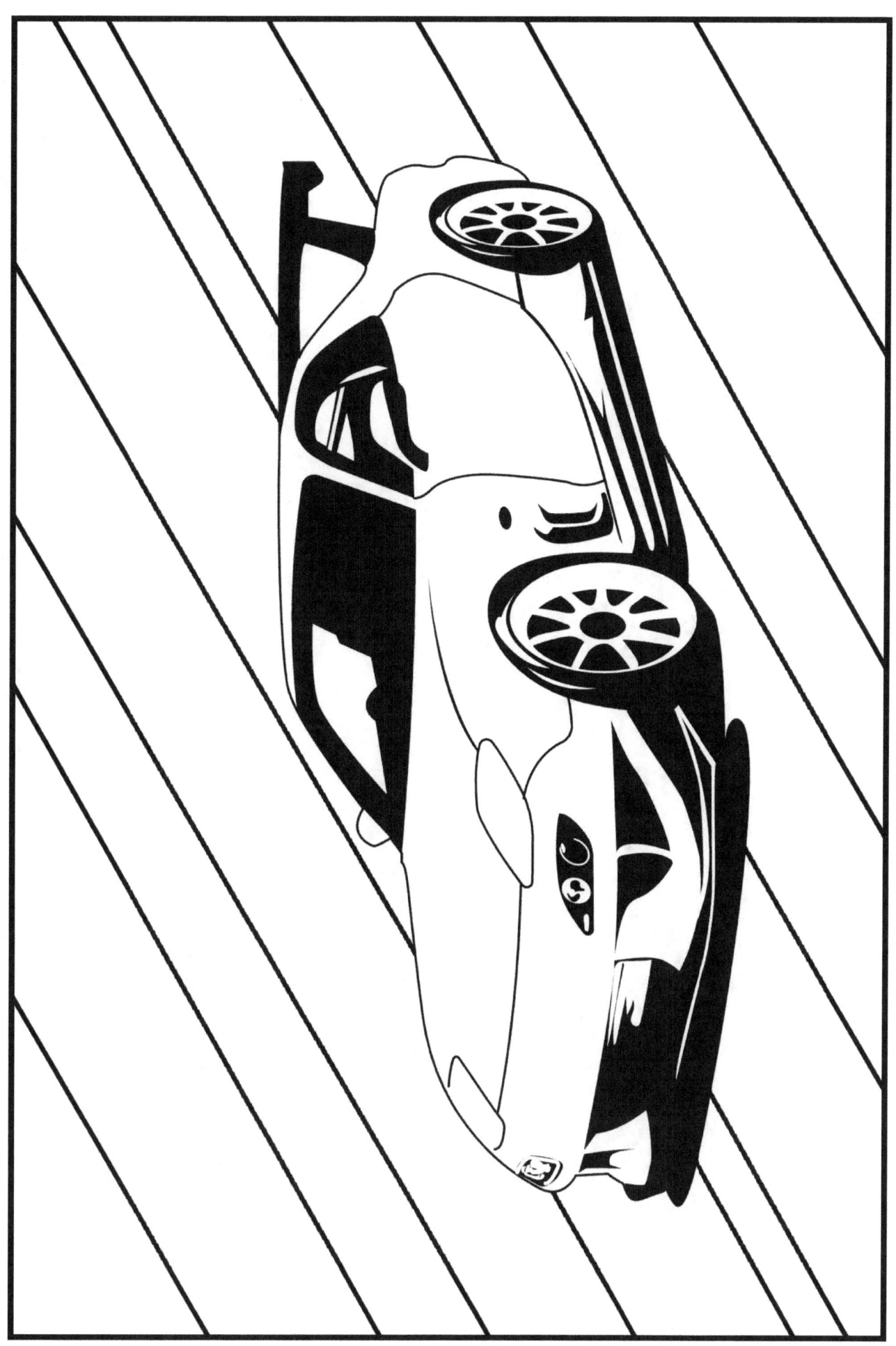

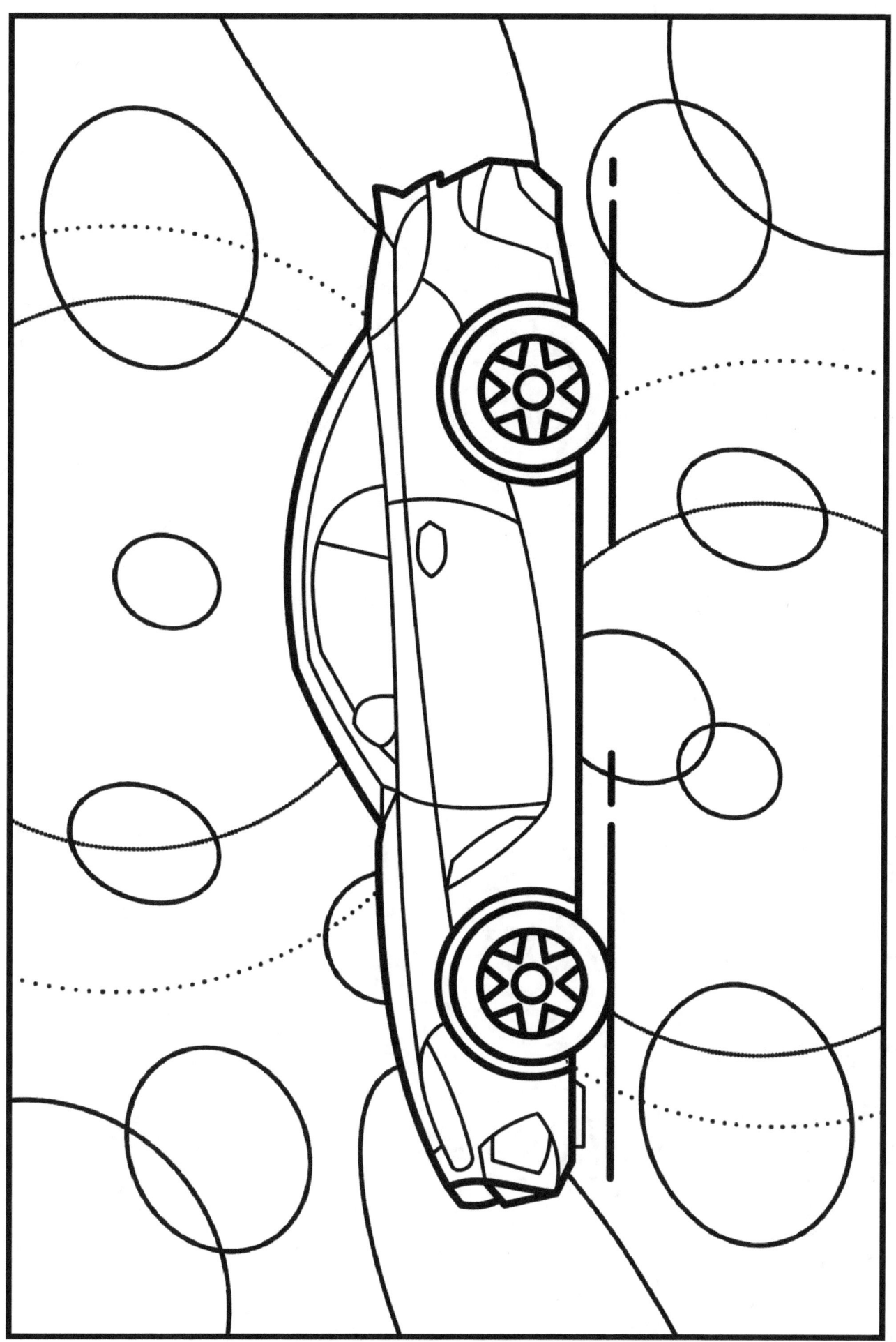

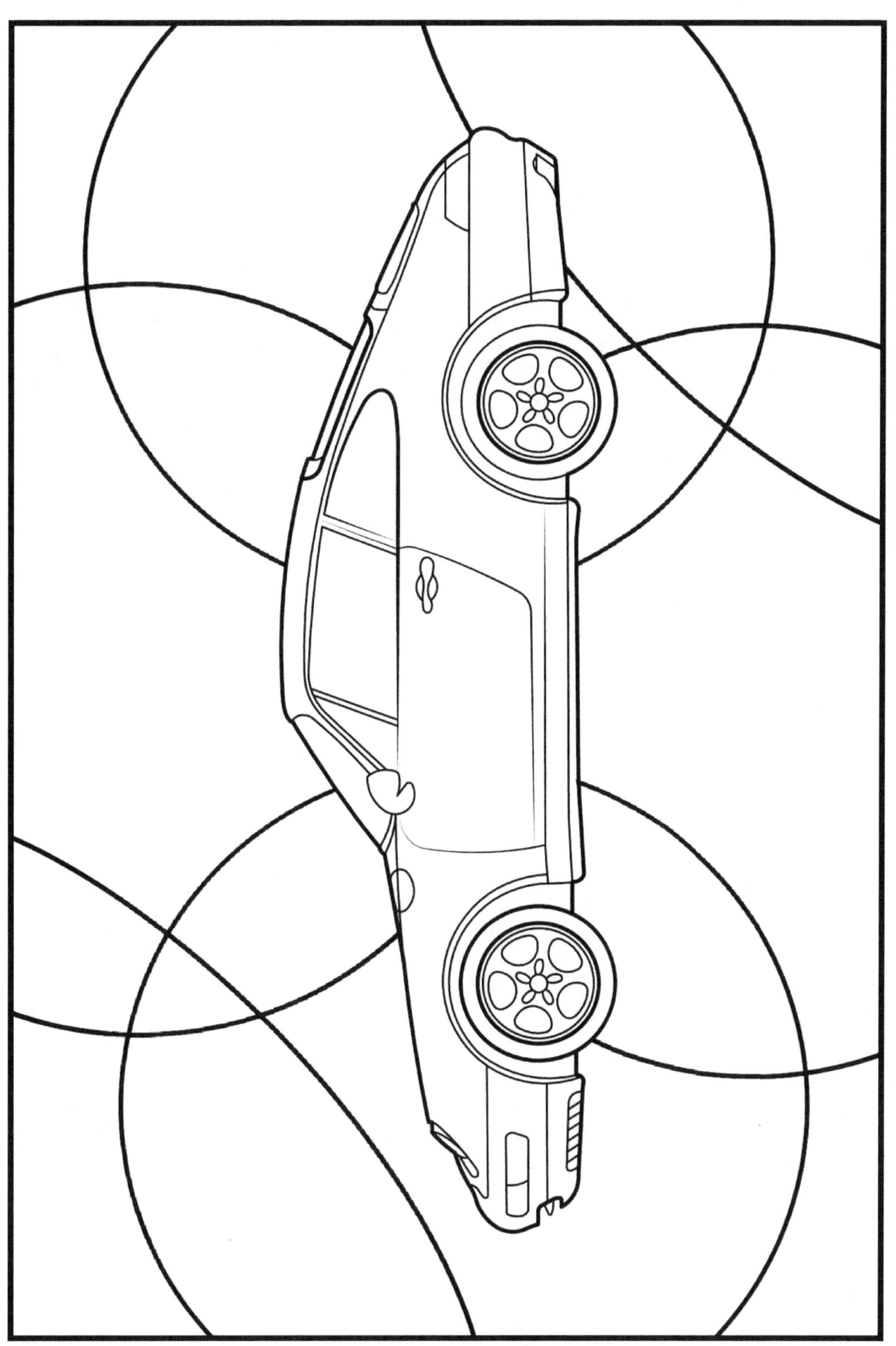

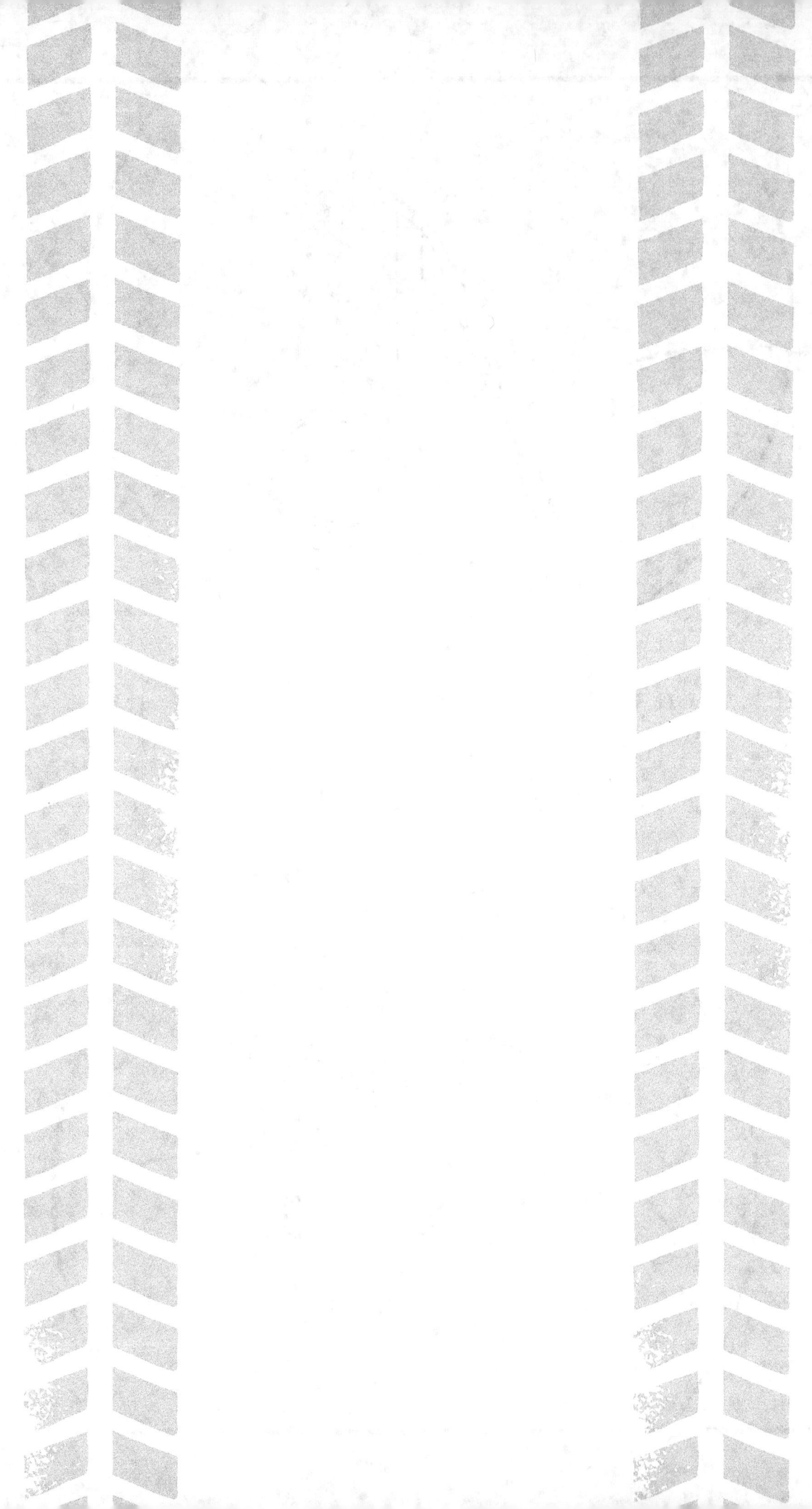

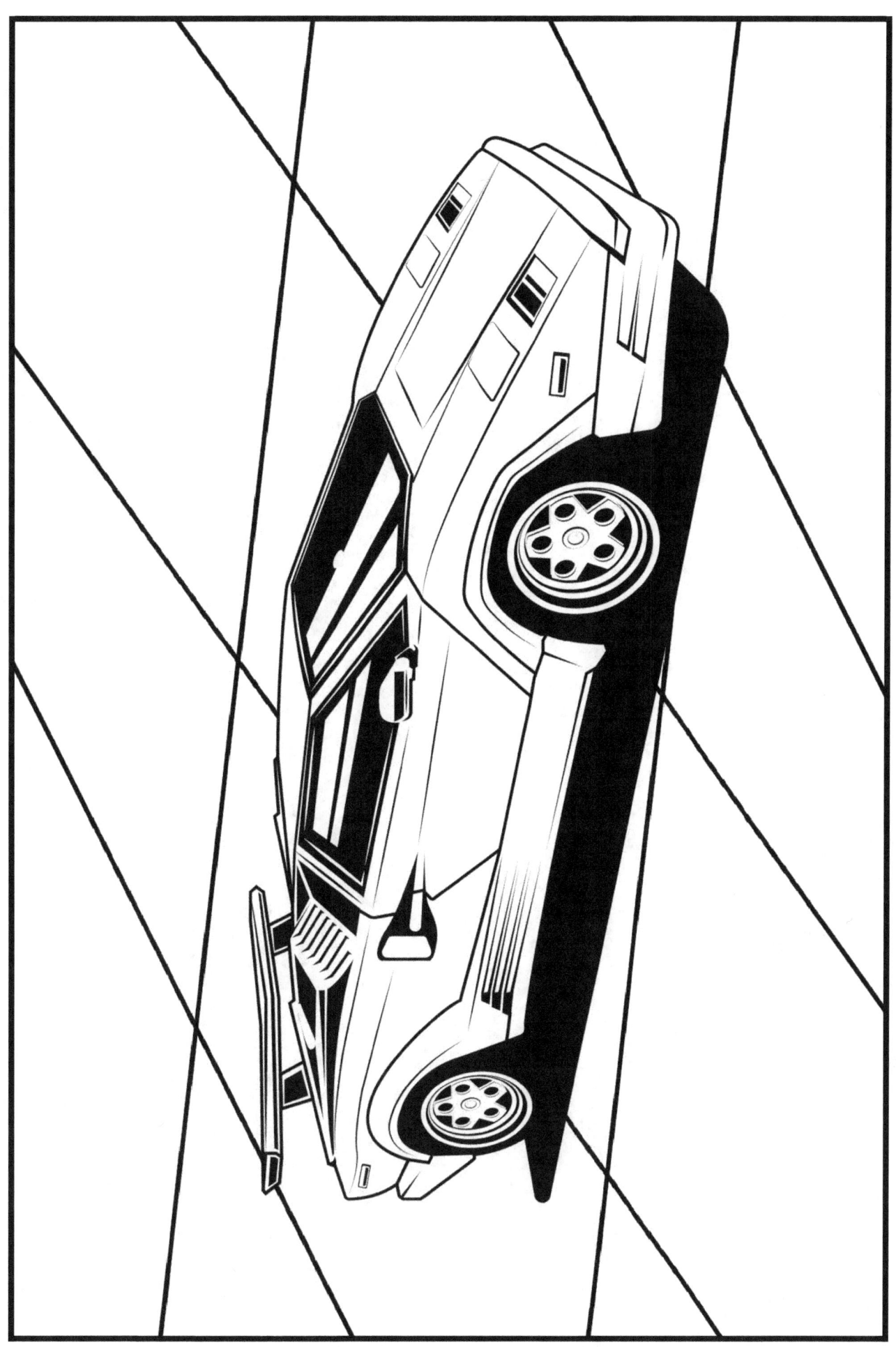

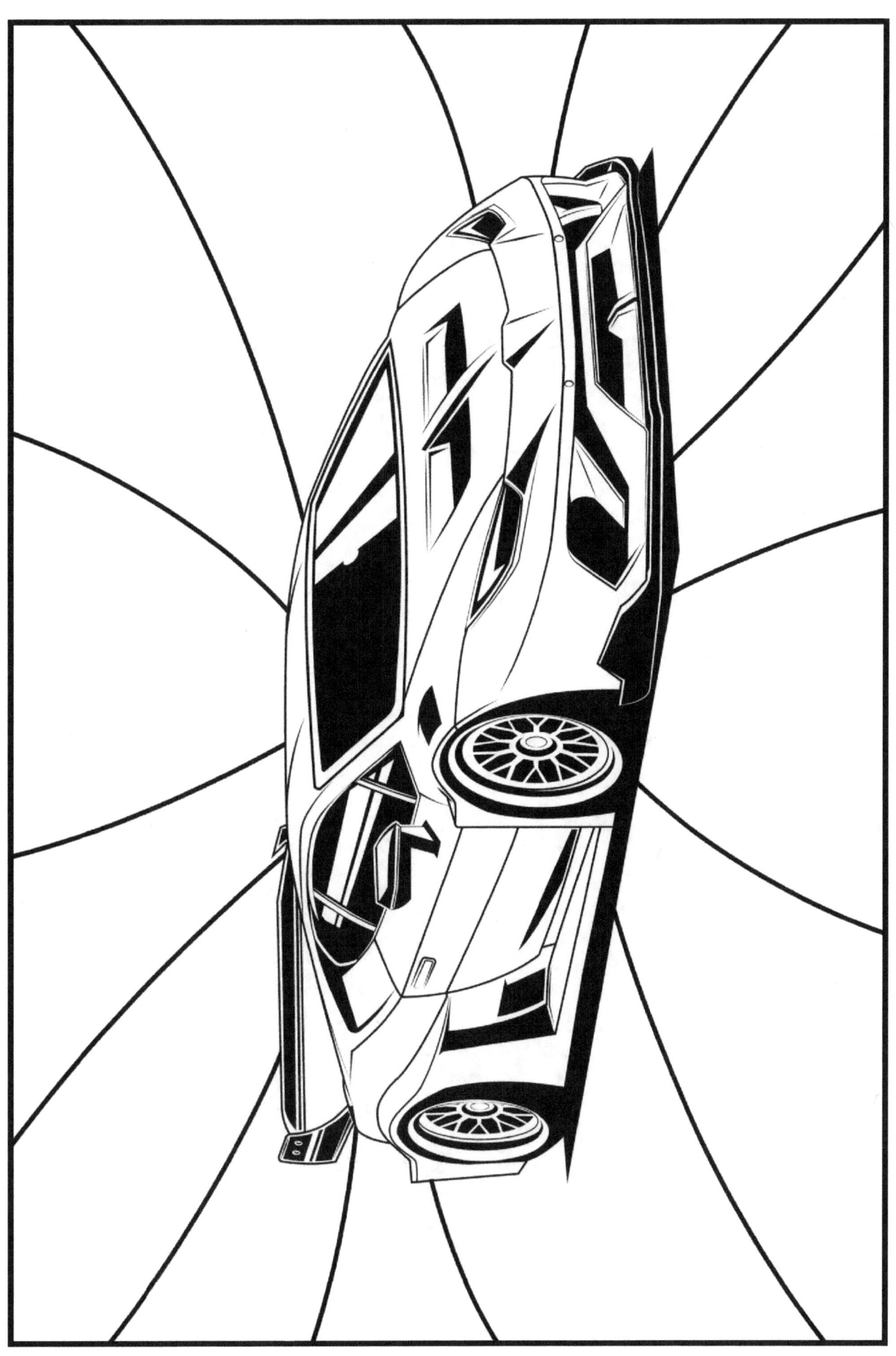

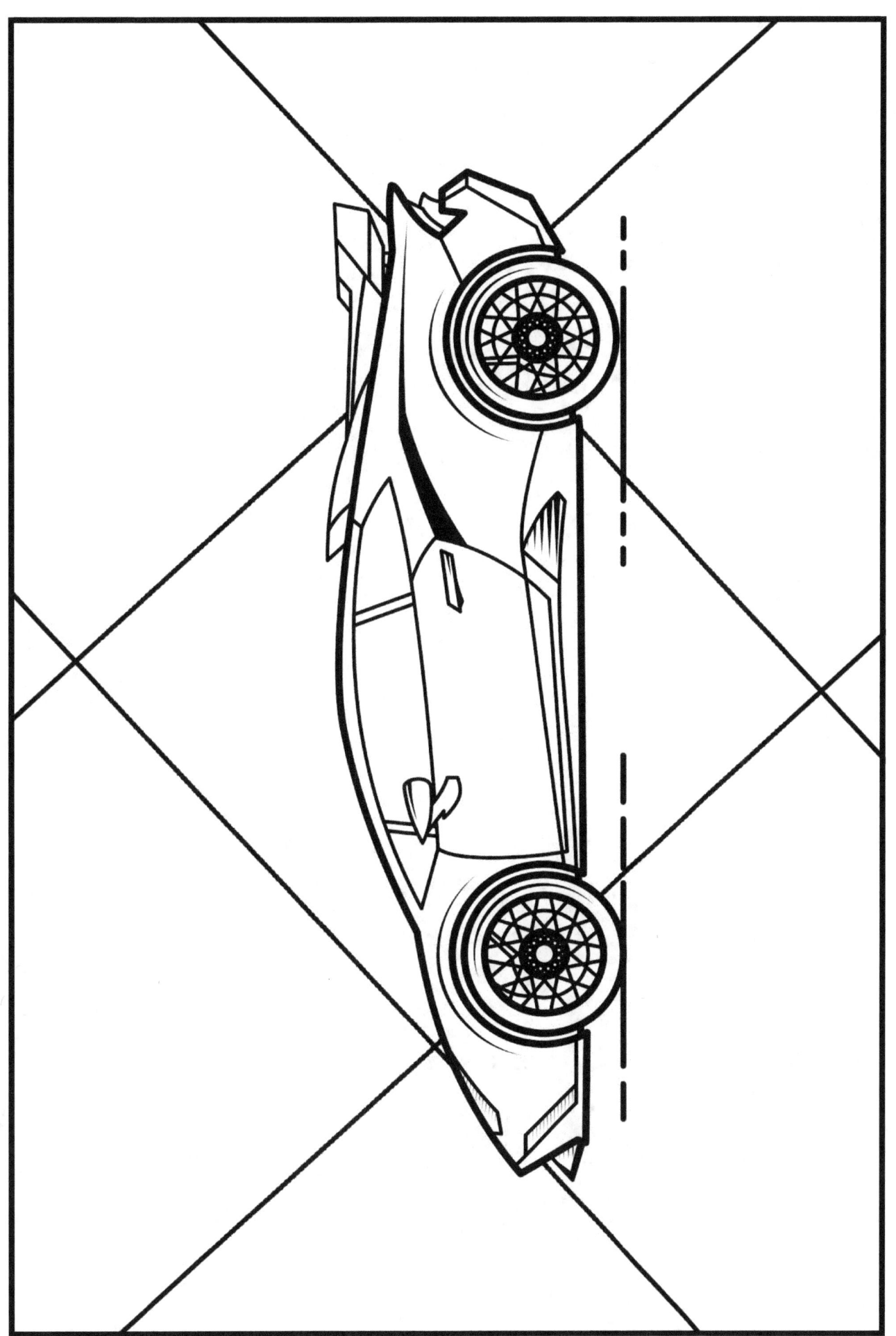

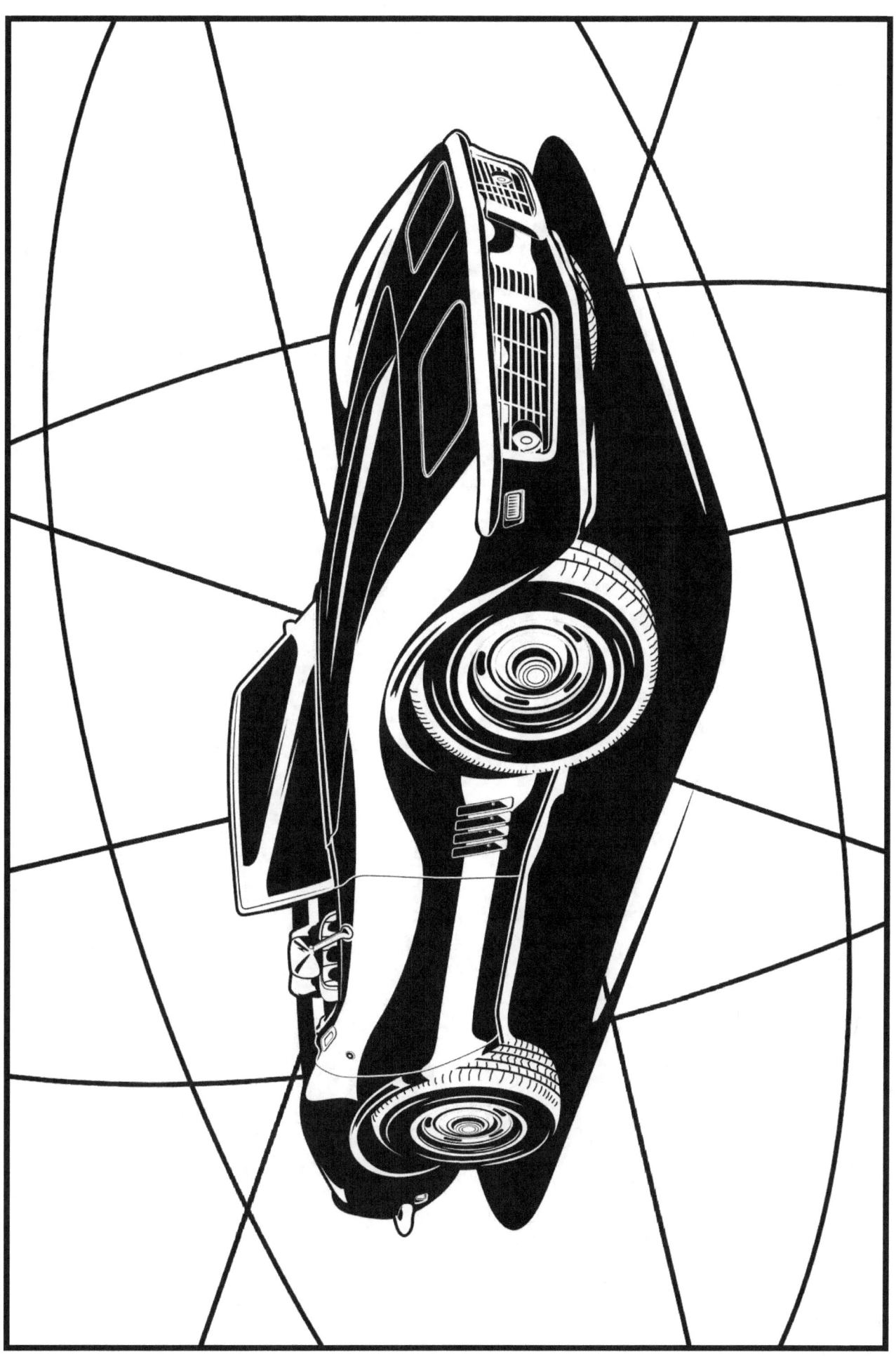

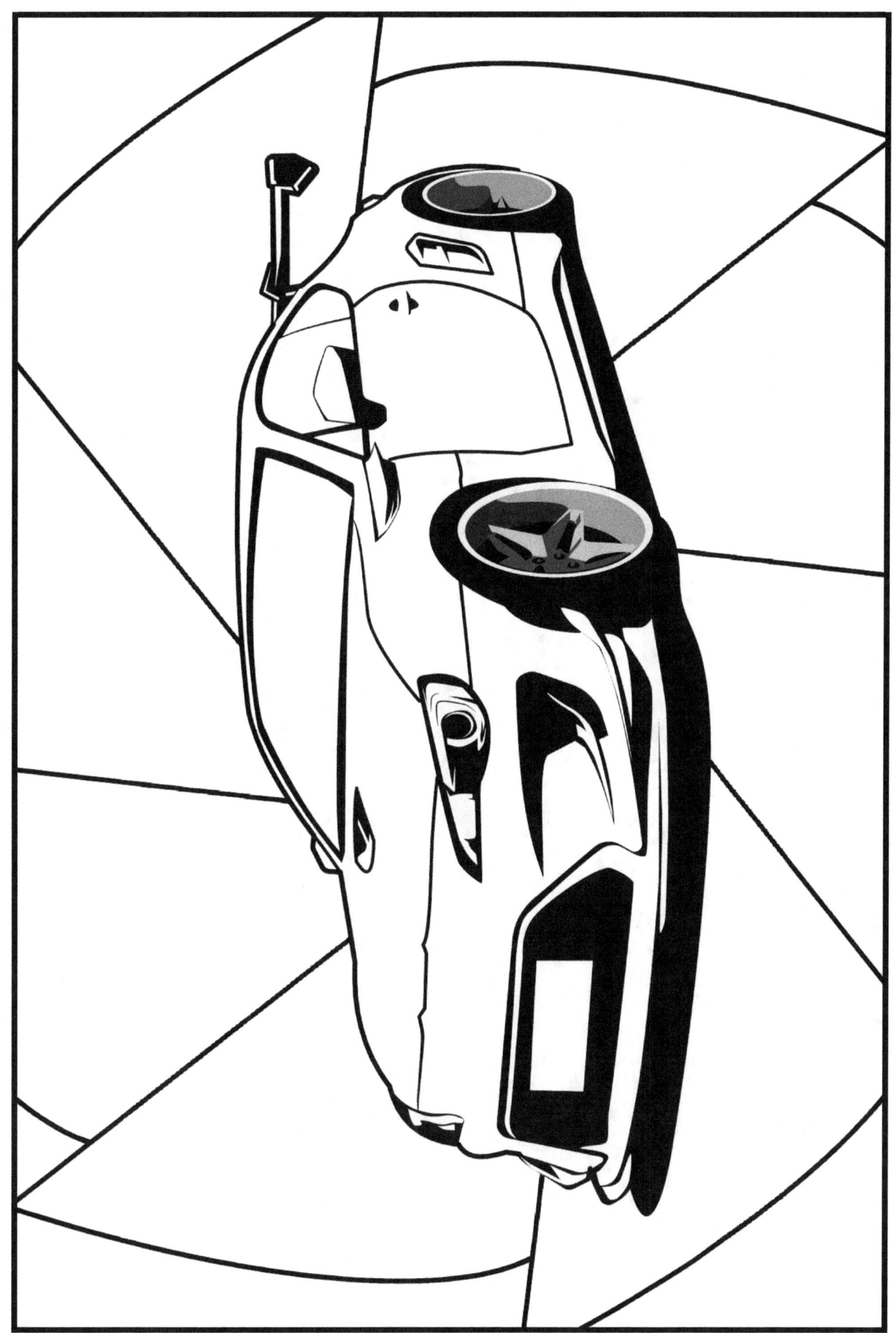

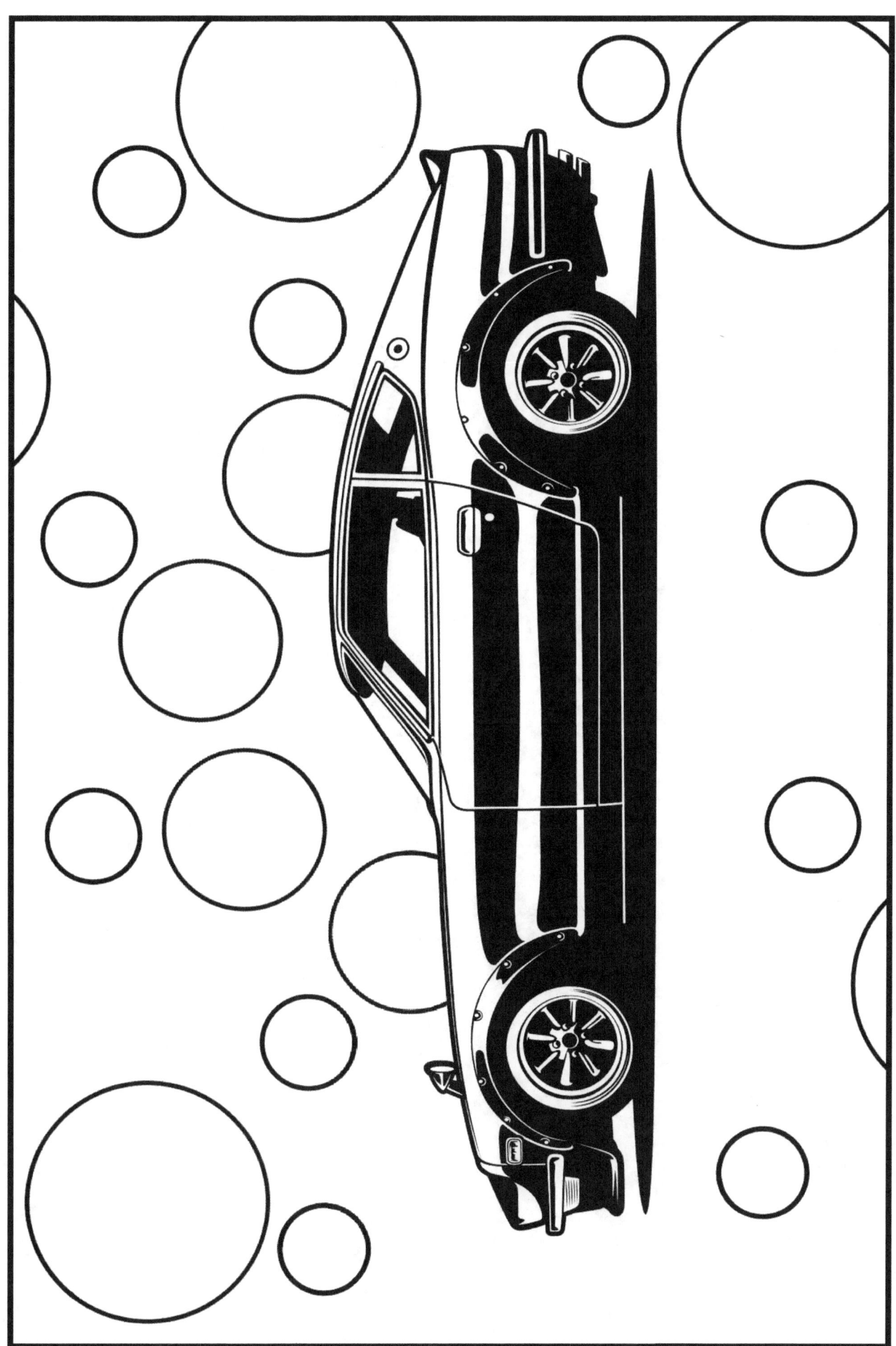

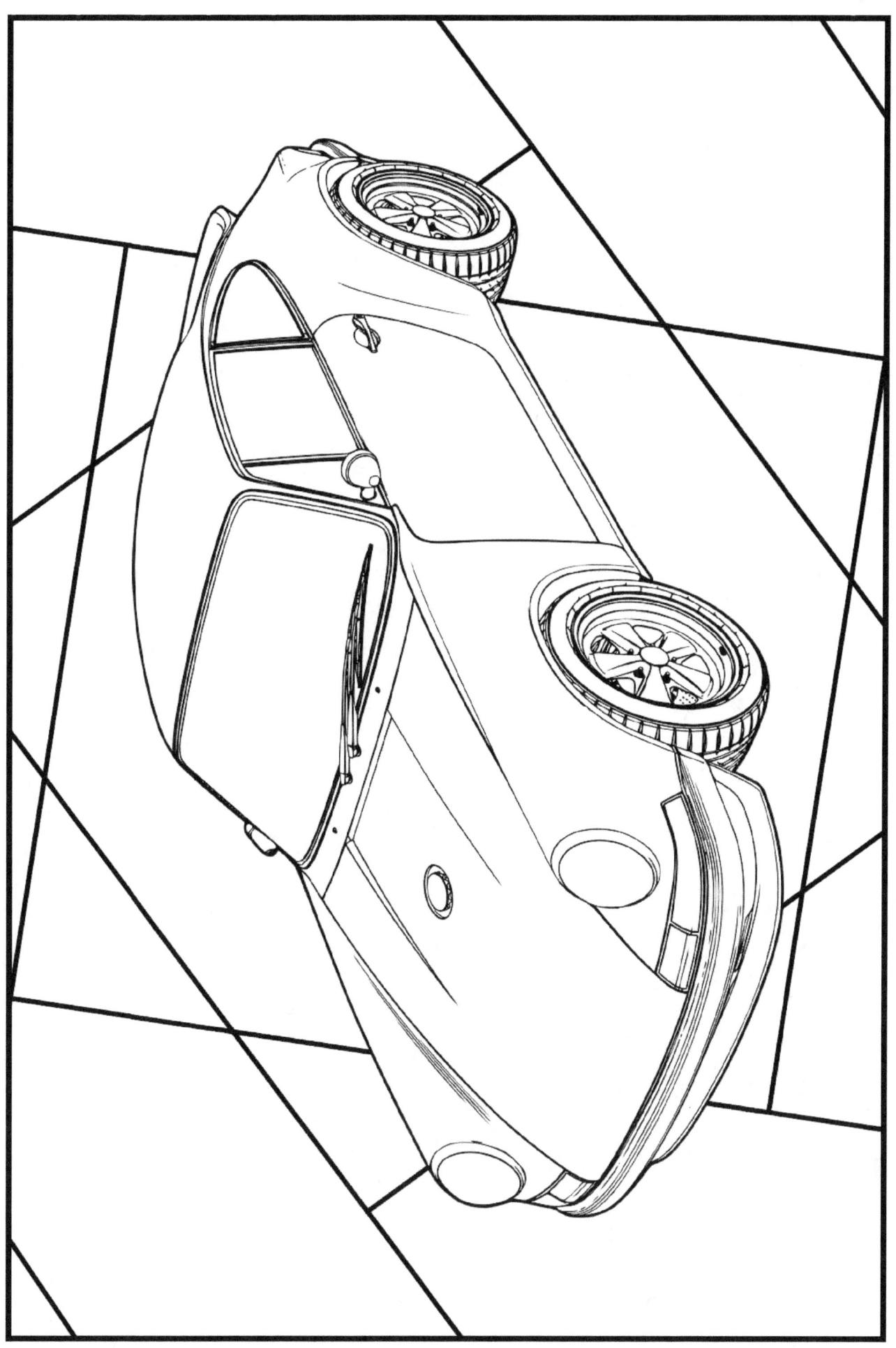

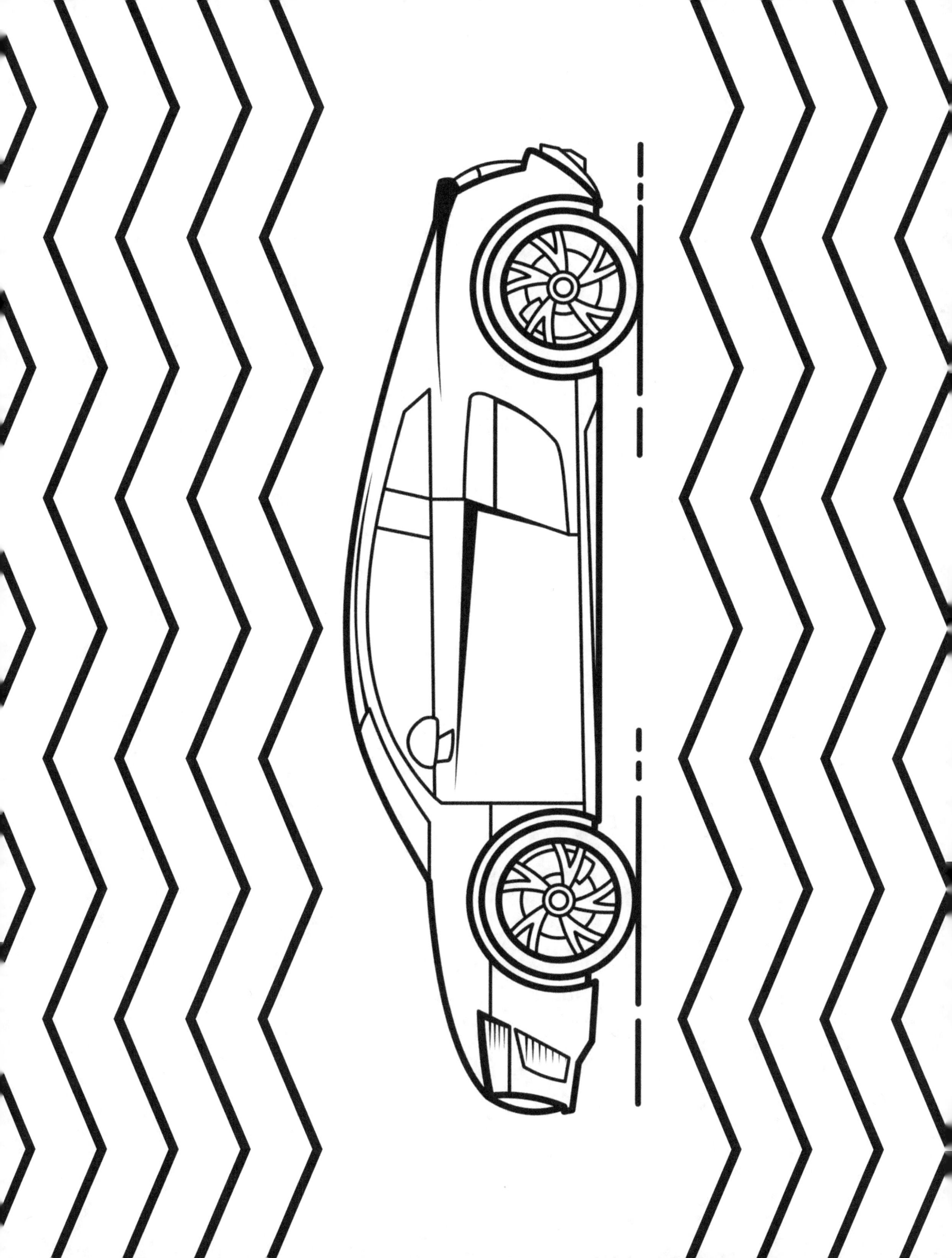

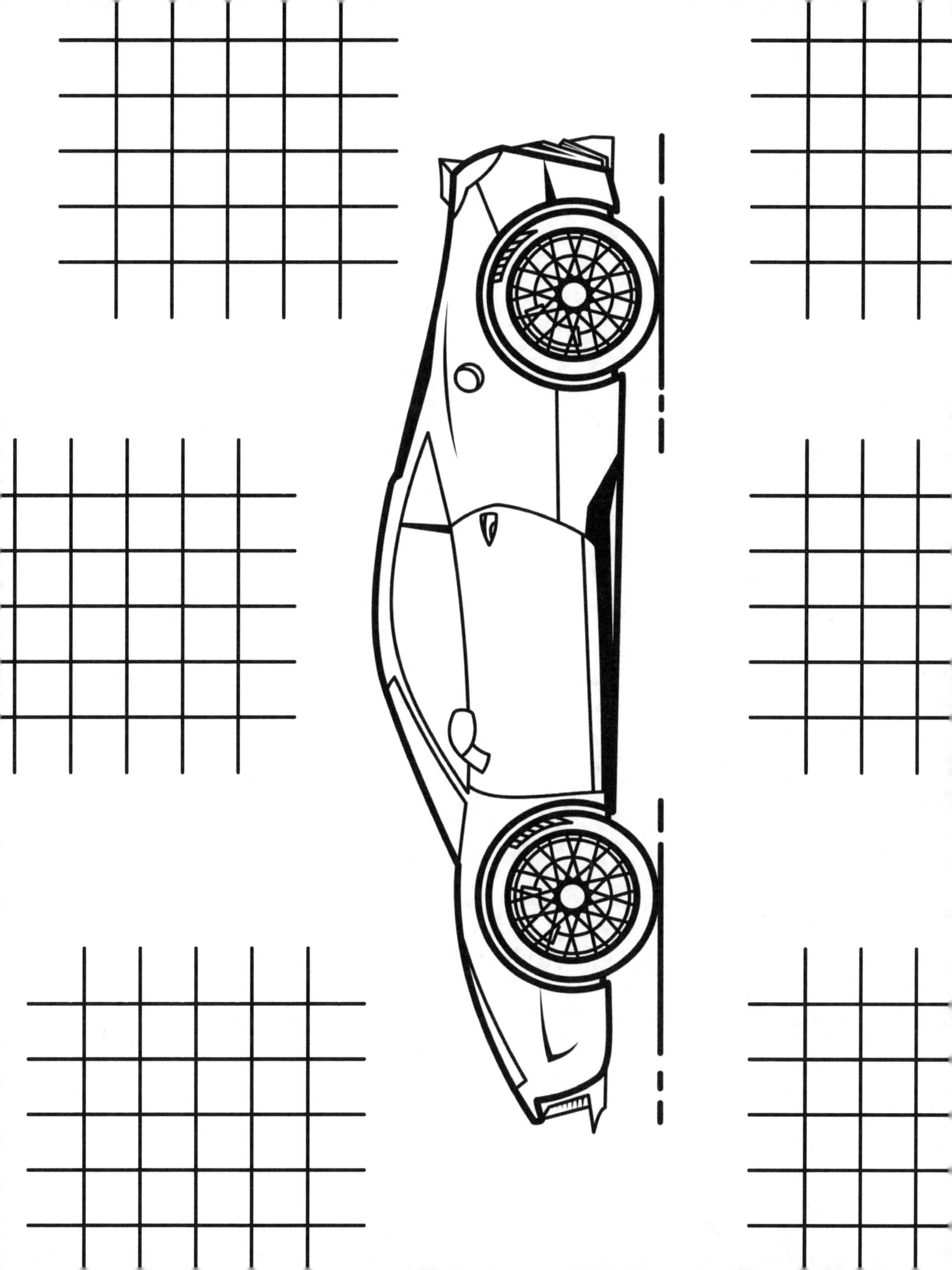

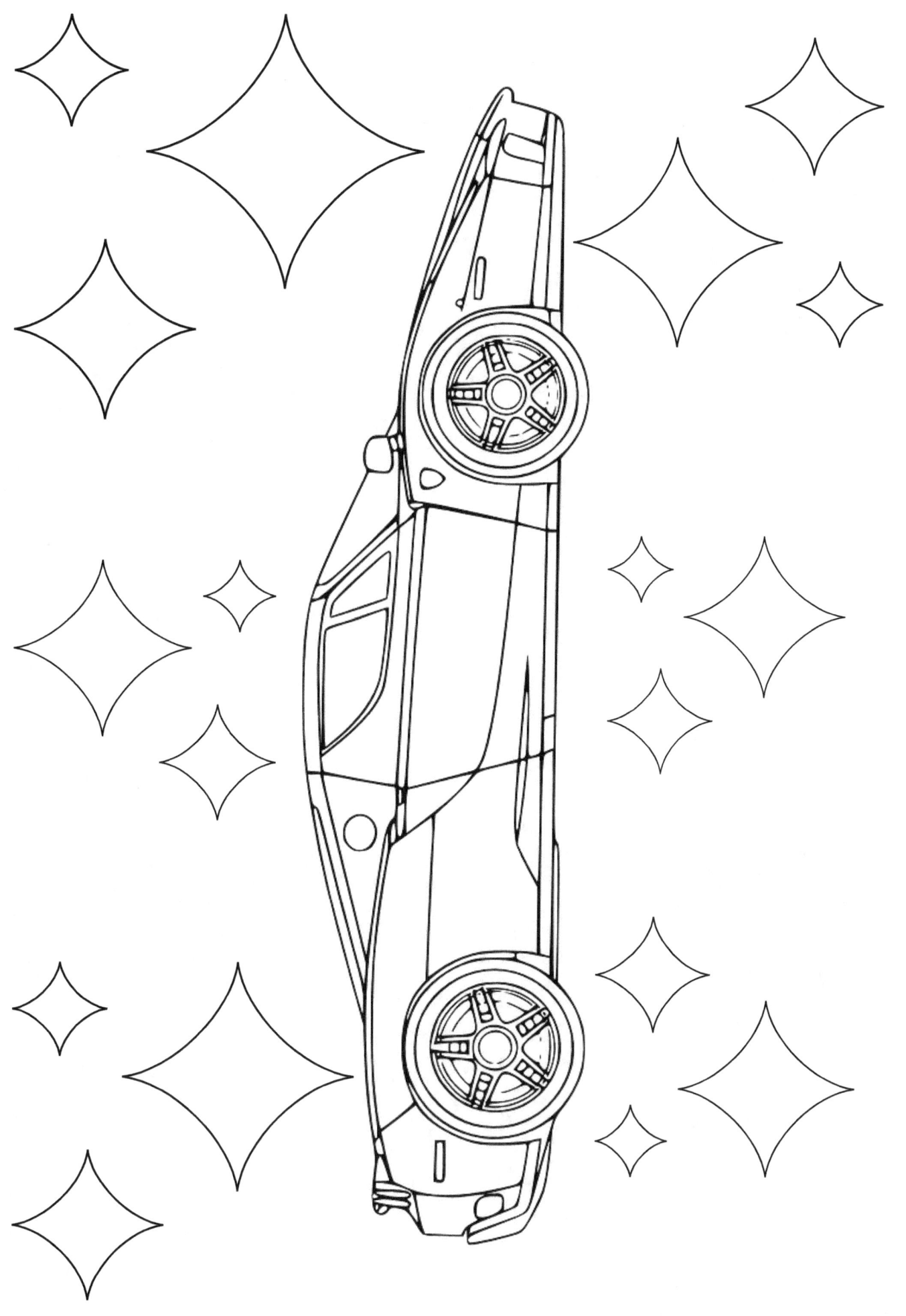

MAKE A U-TURN FOR MUSCLE CARS COLORING PAGES

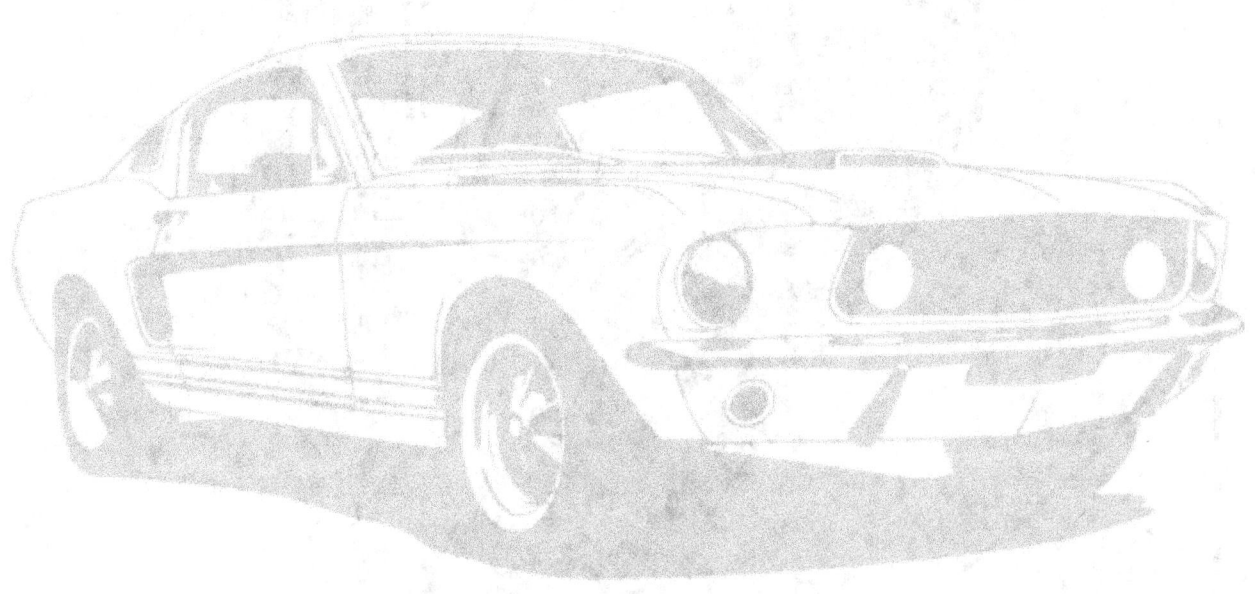

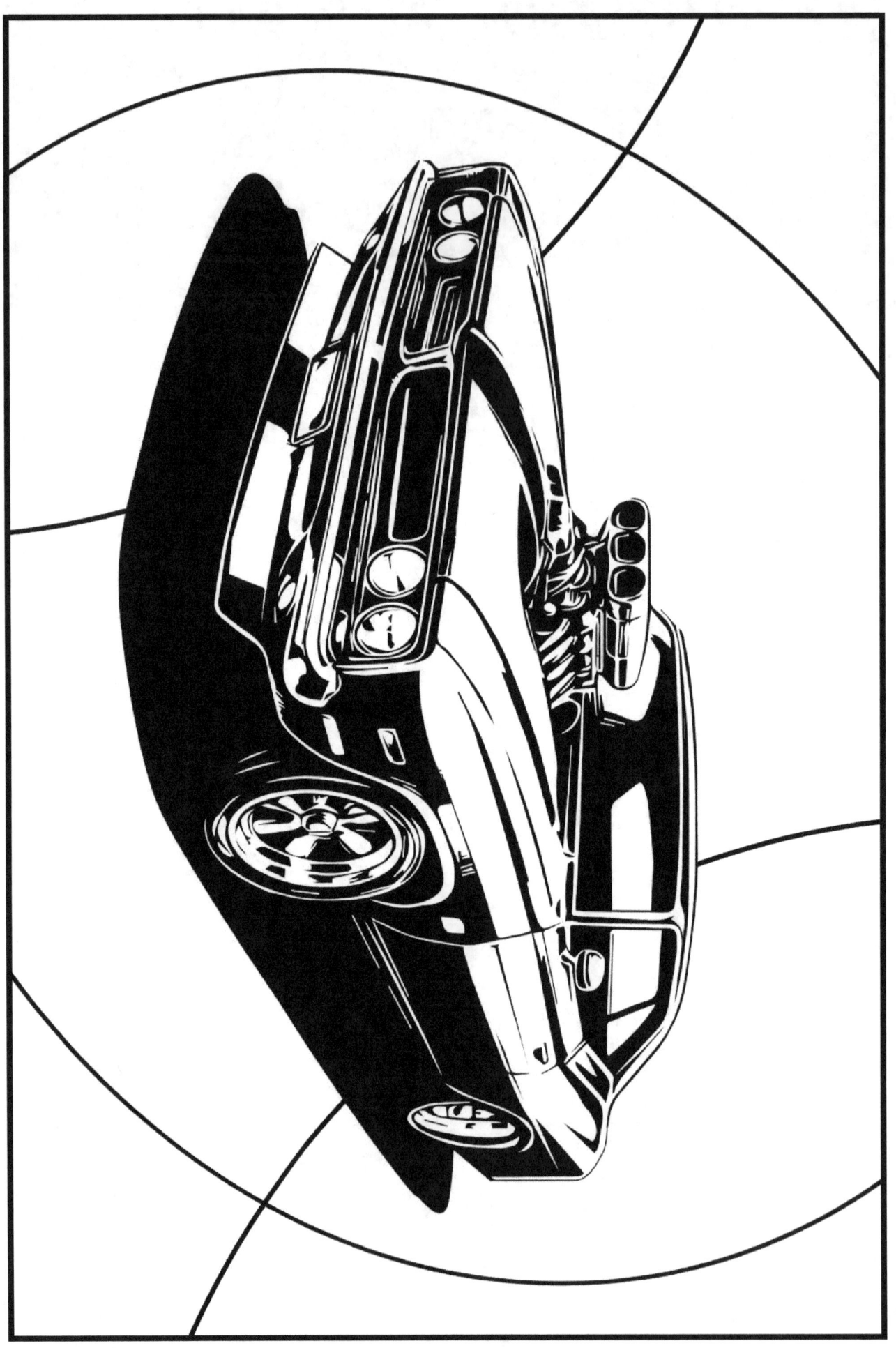

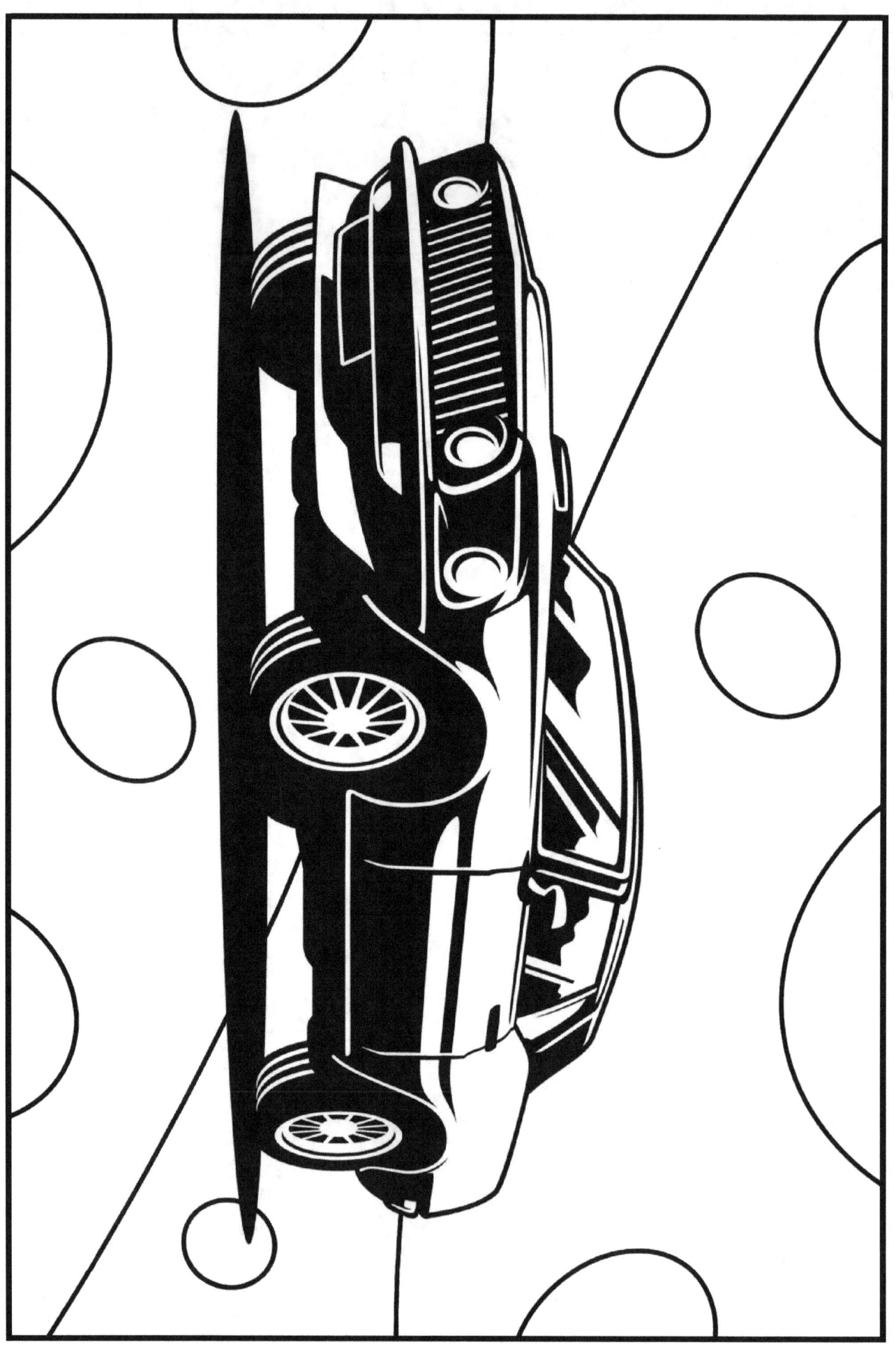

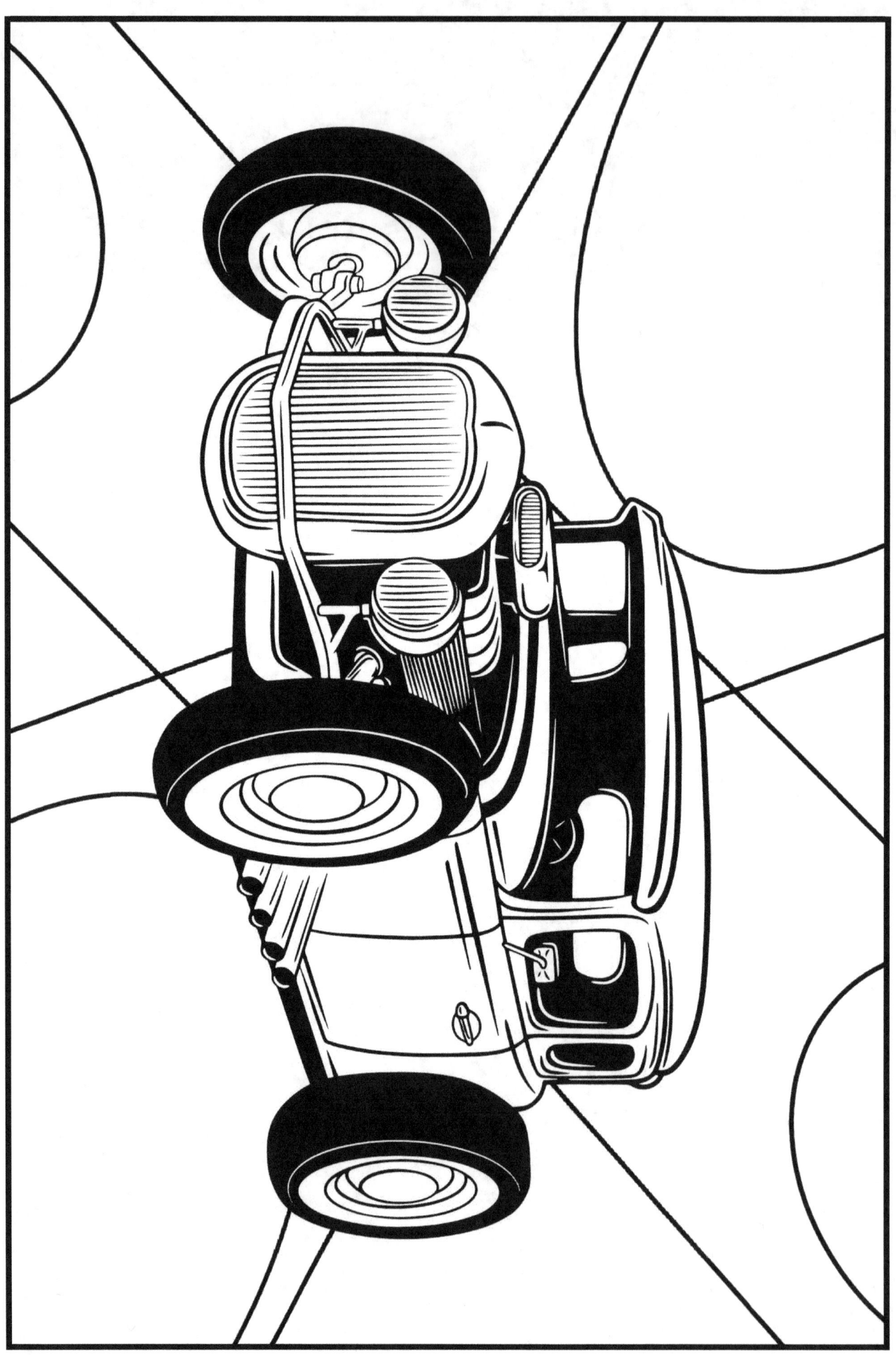

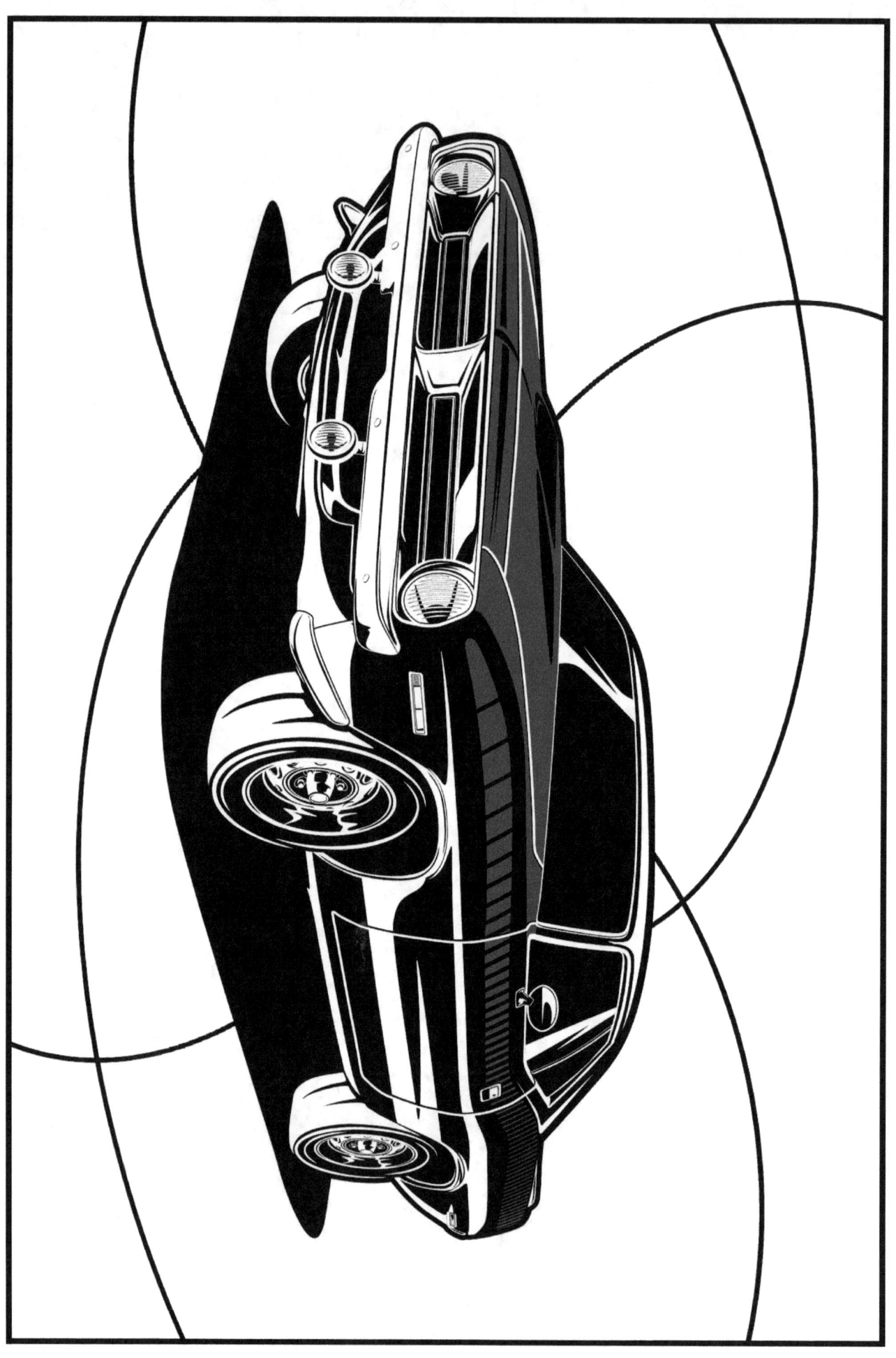

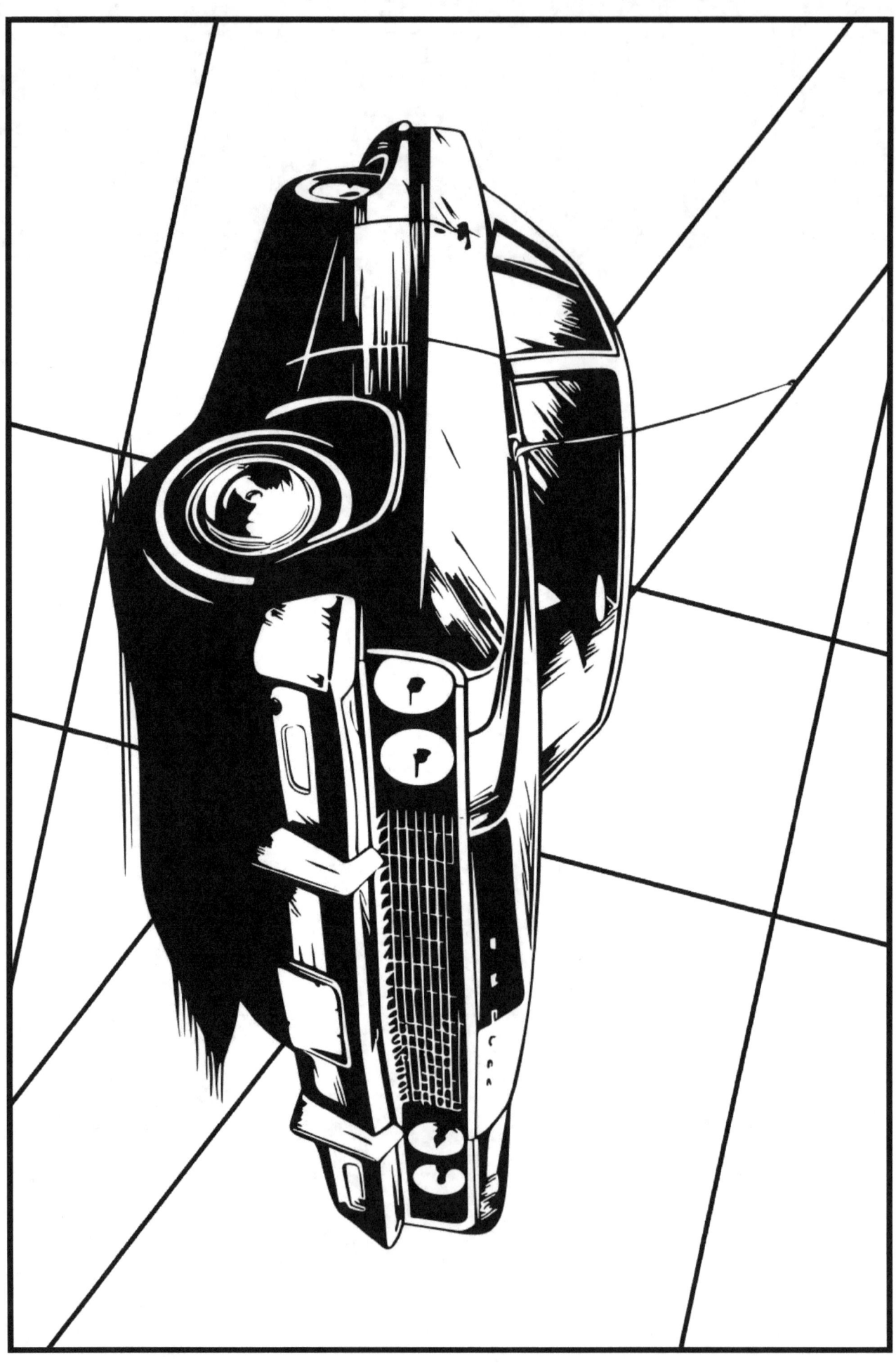

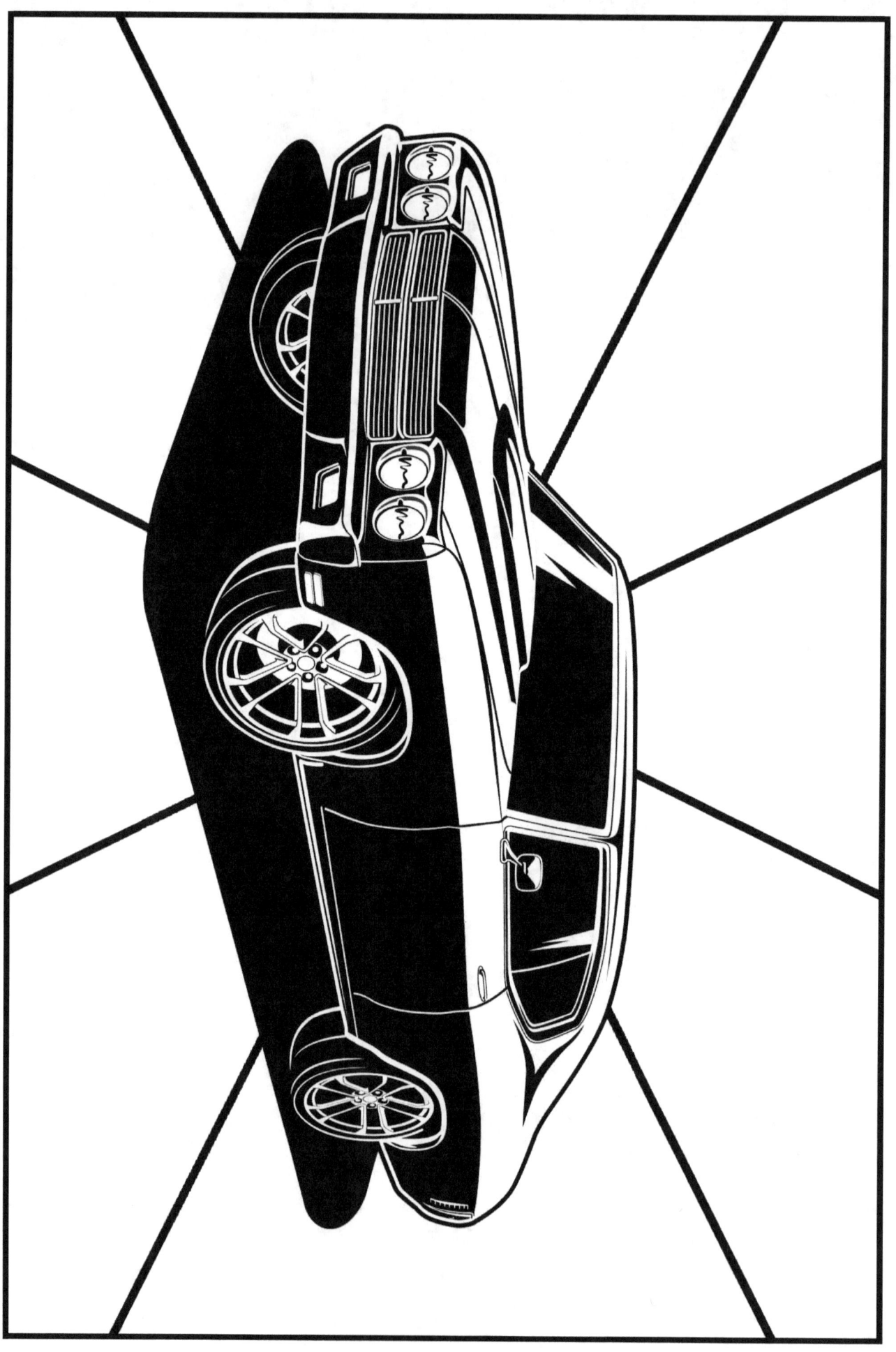

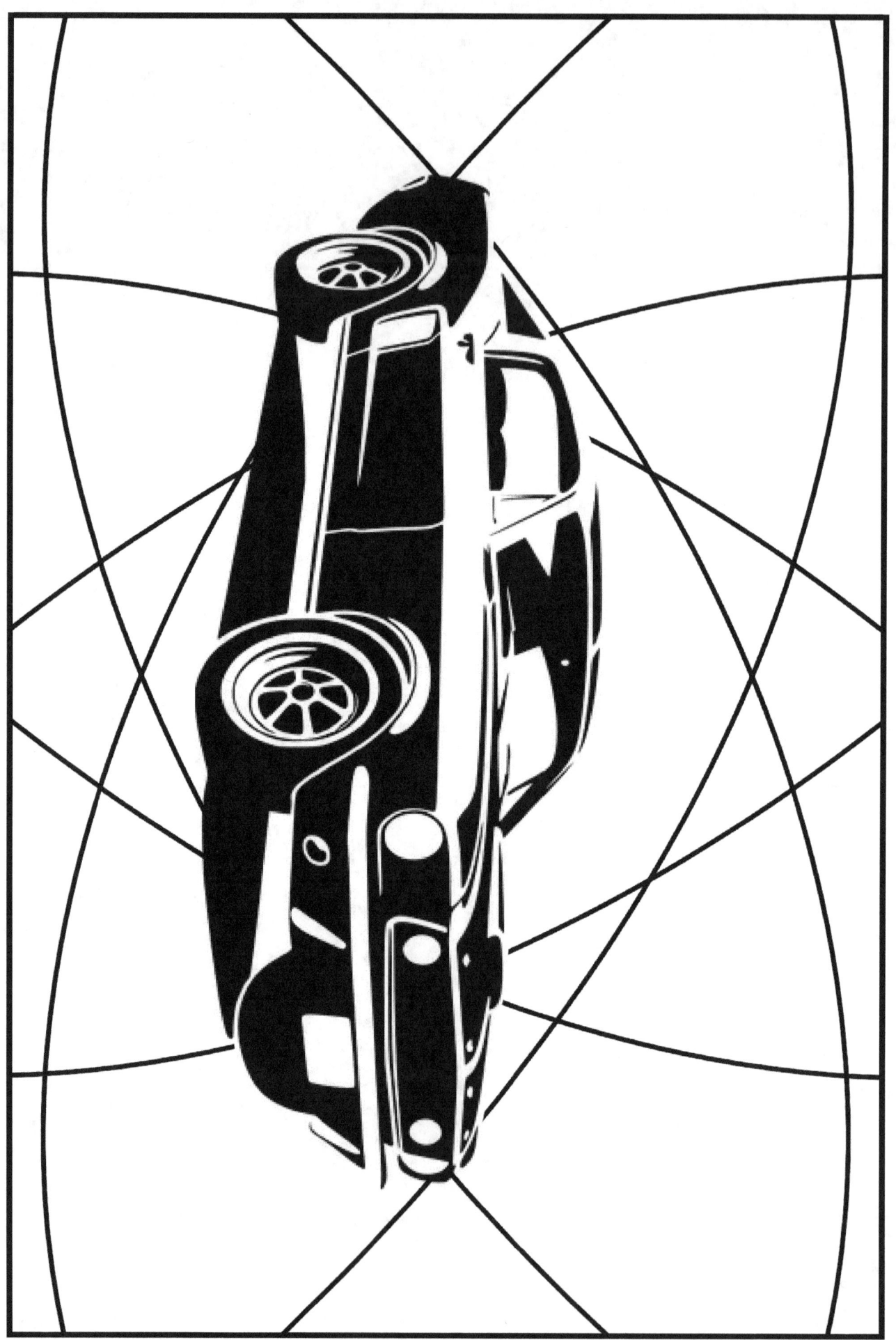

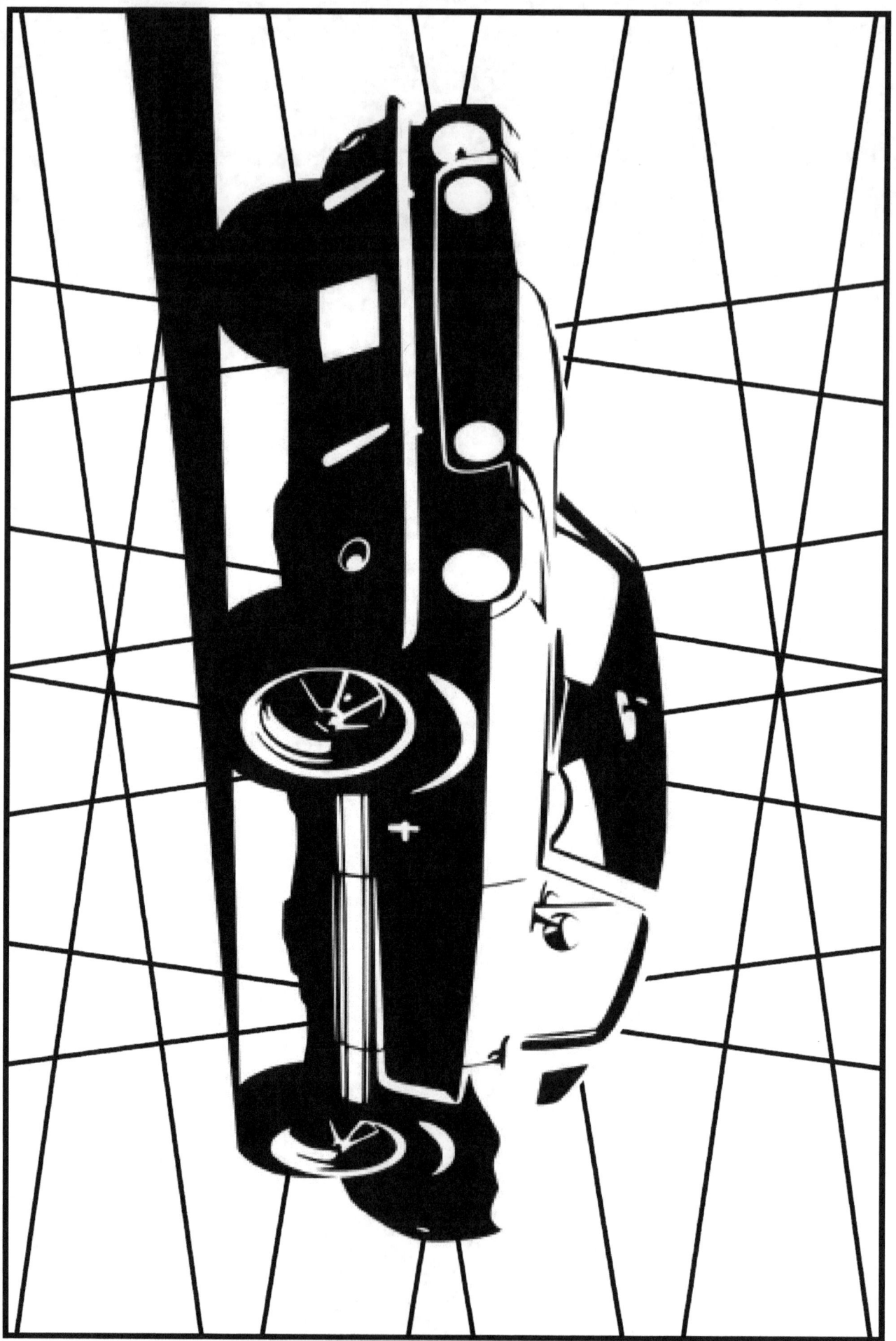

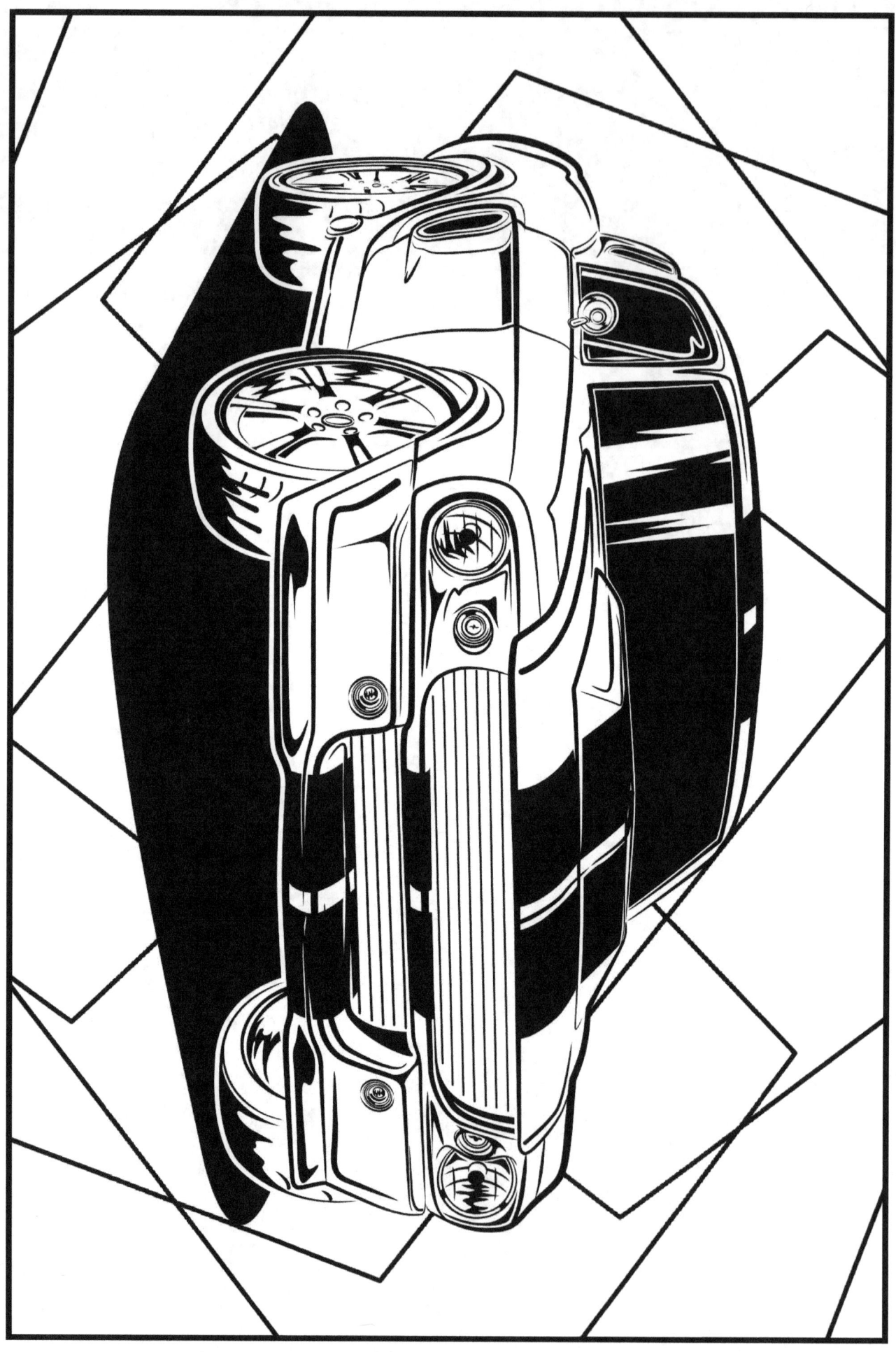

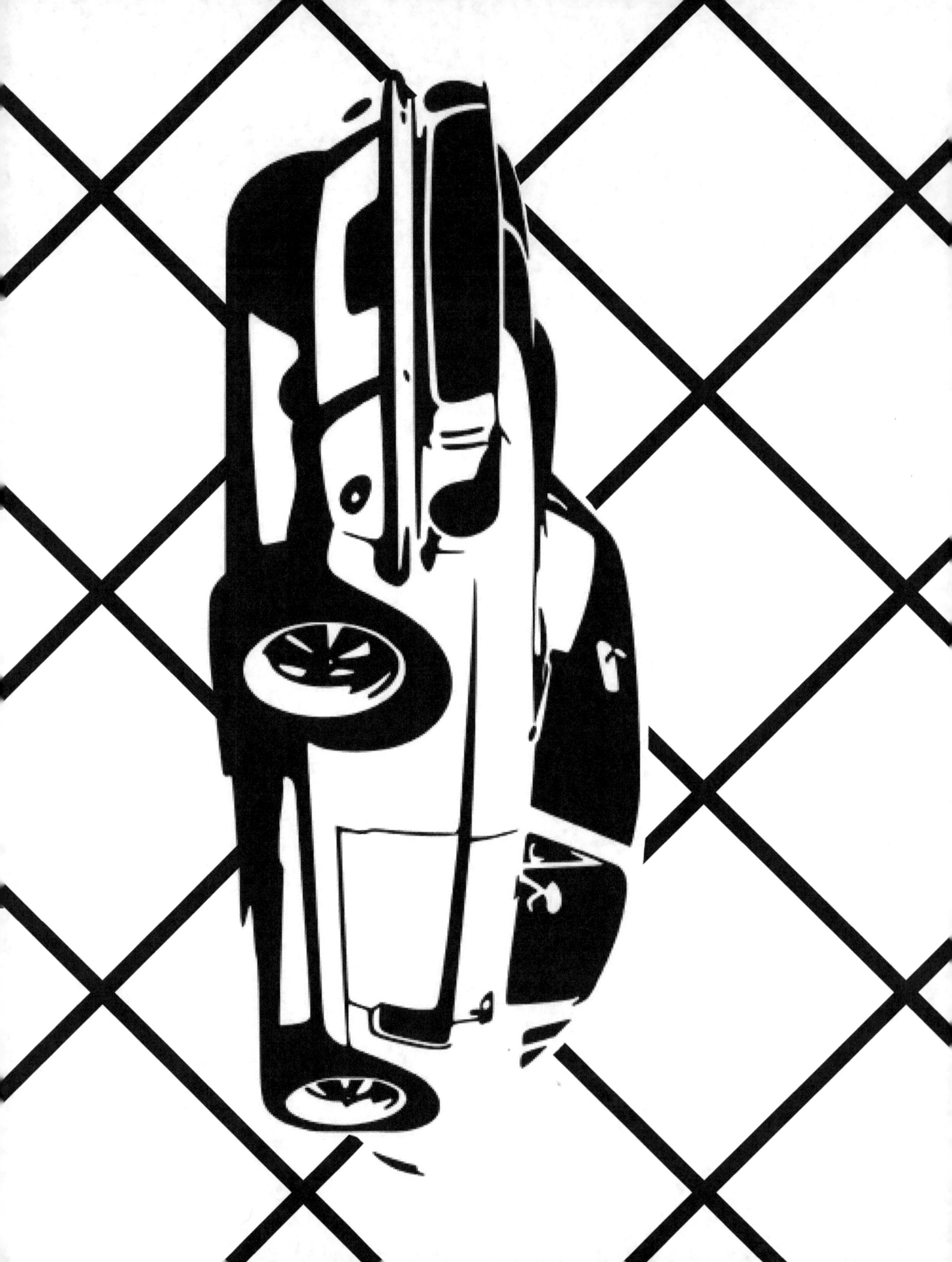

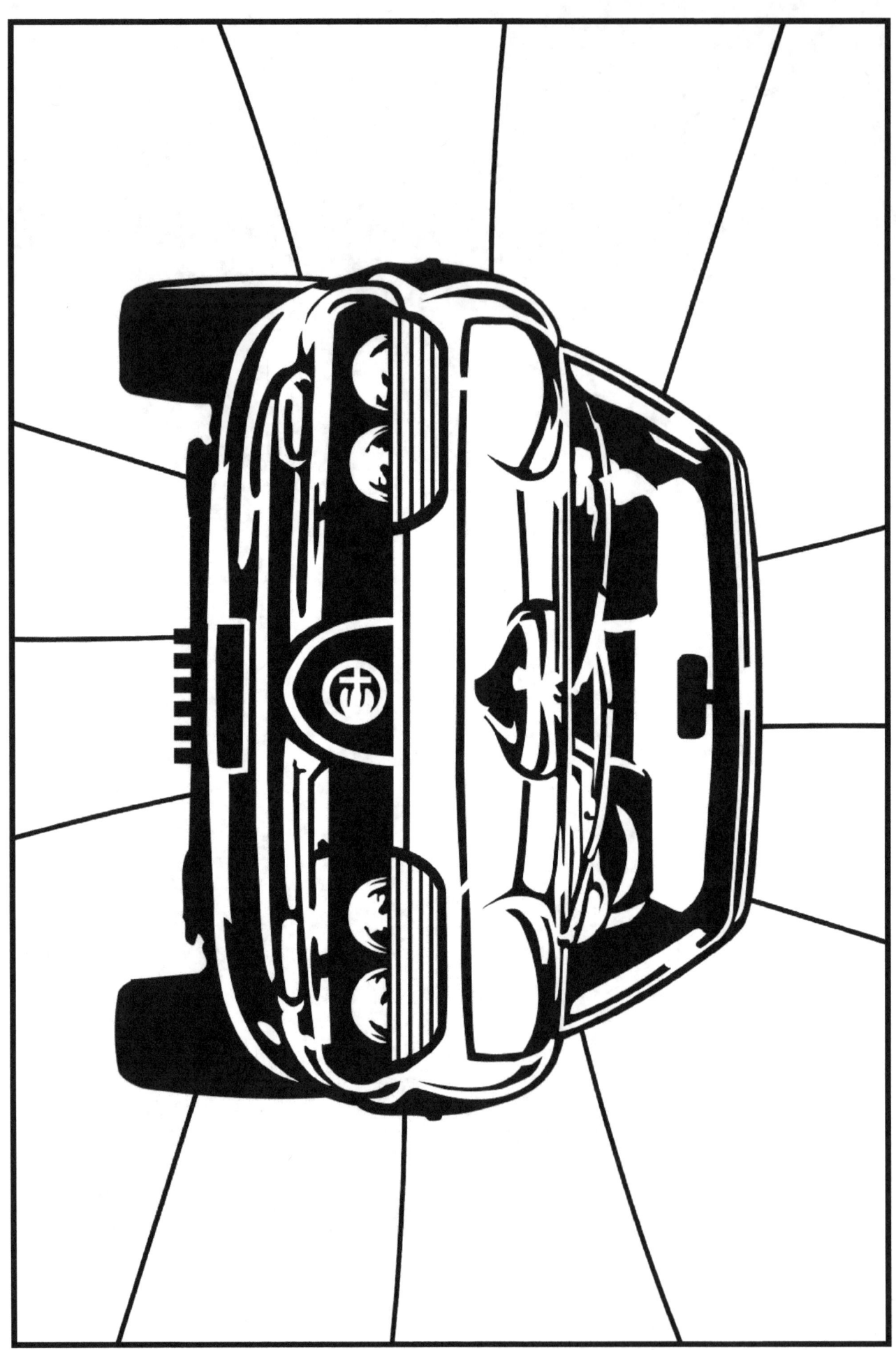

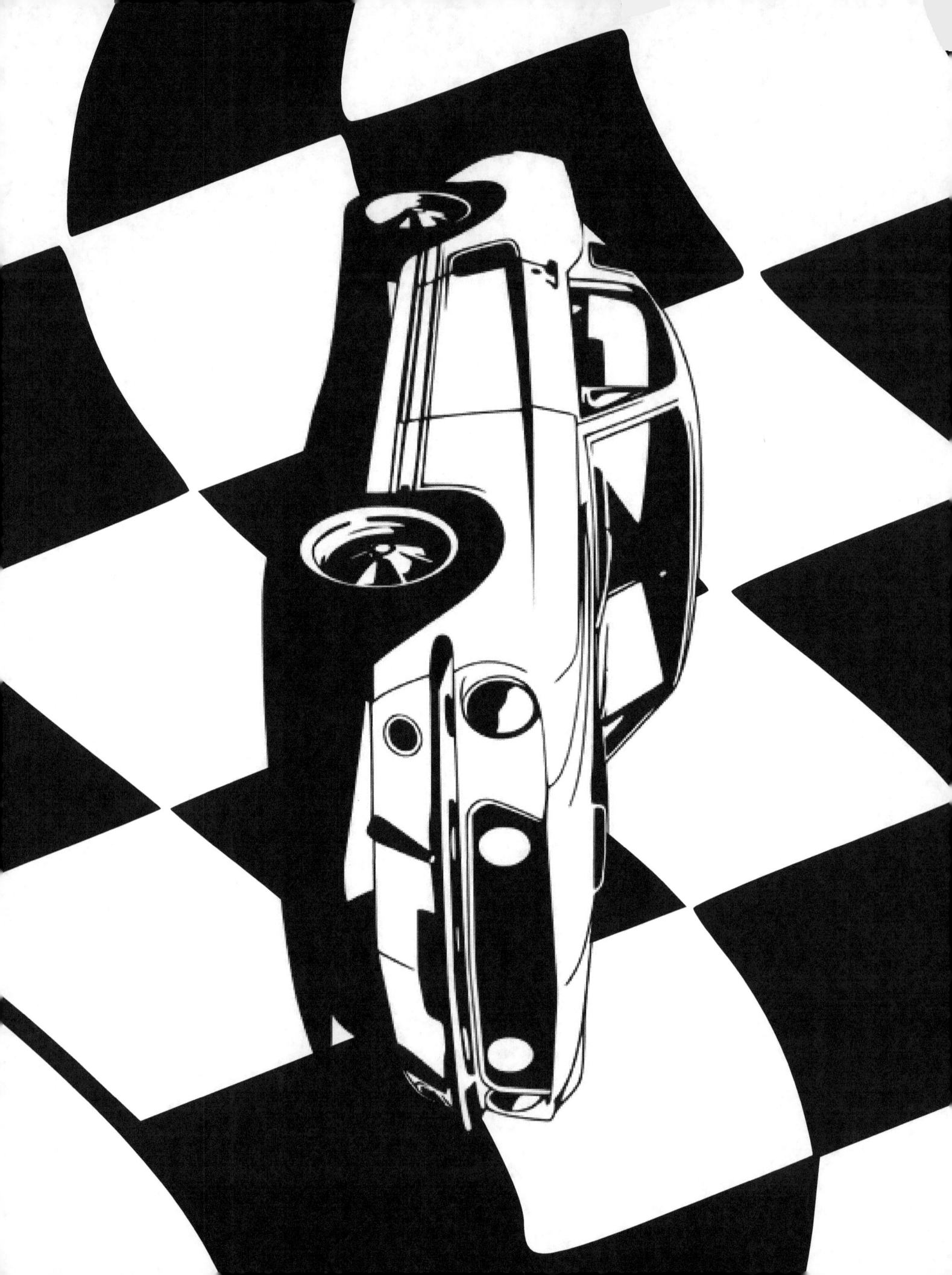

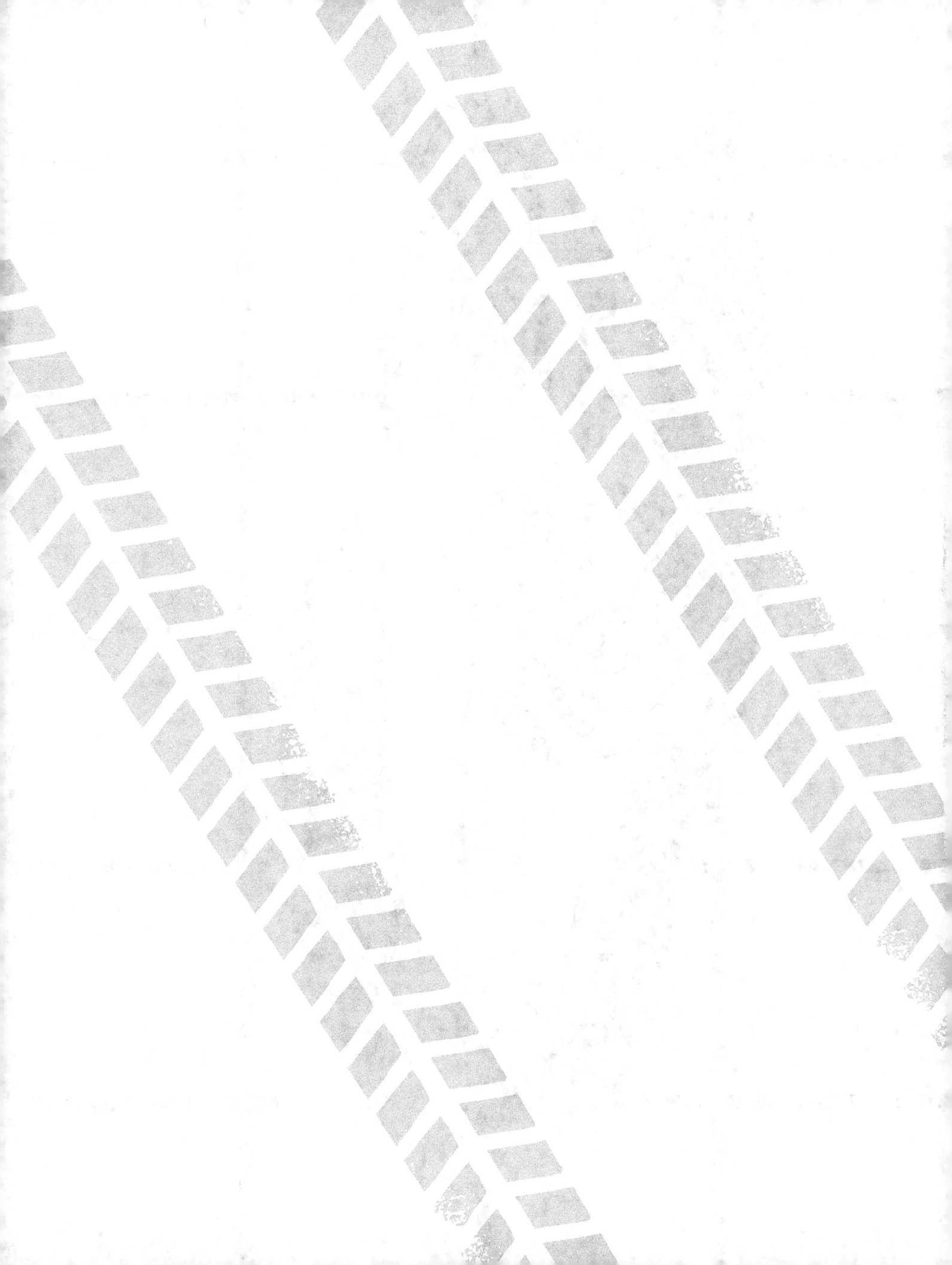

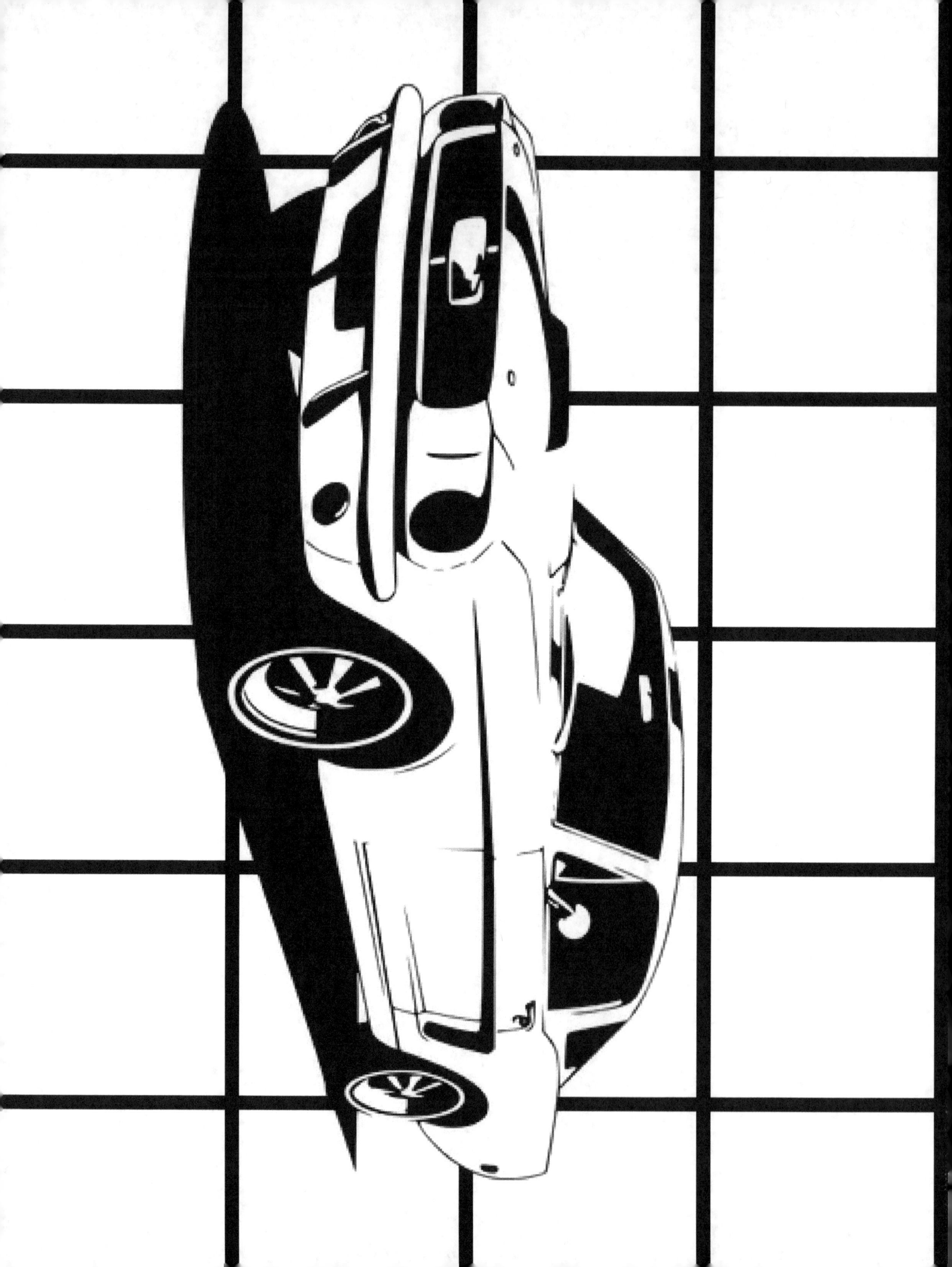

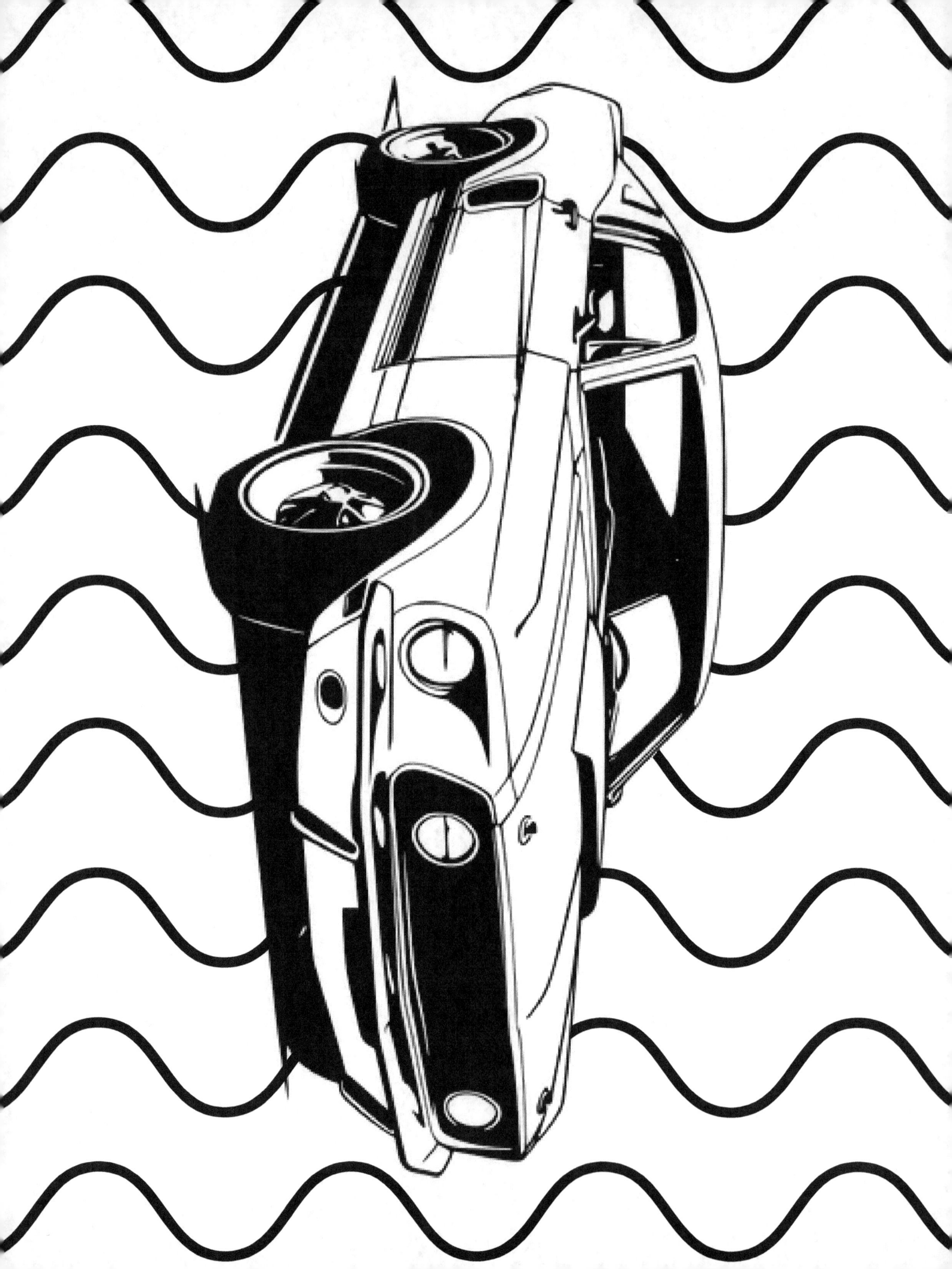

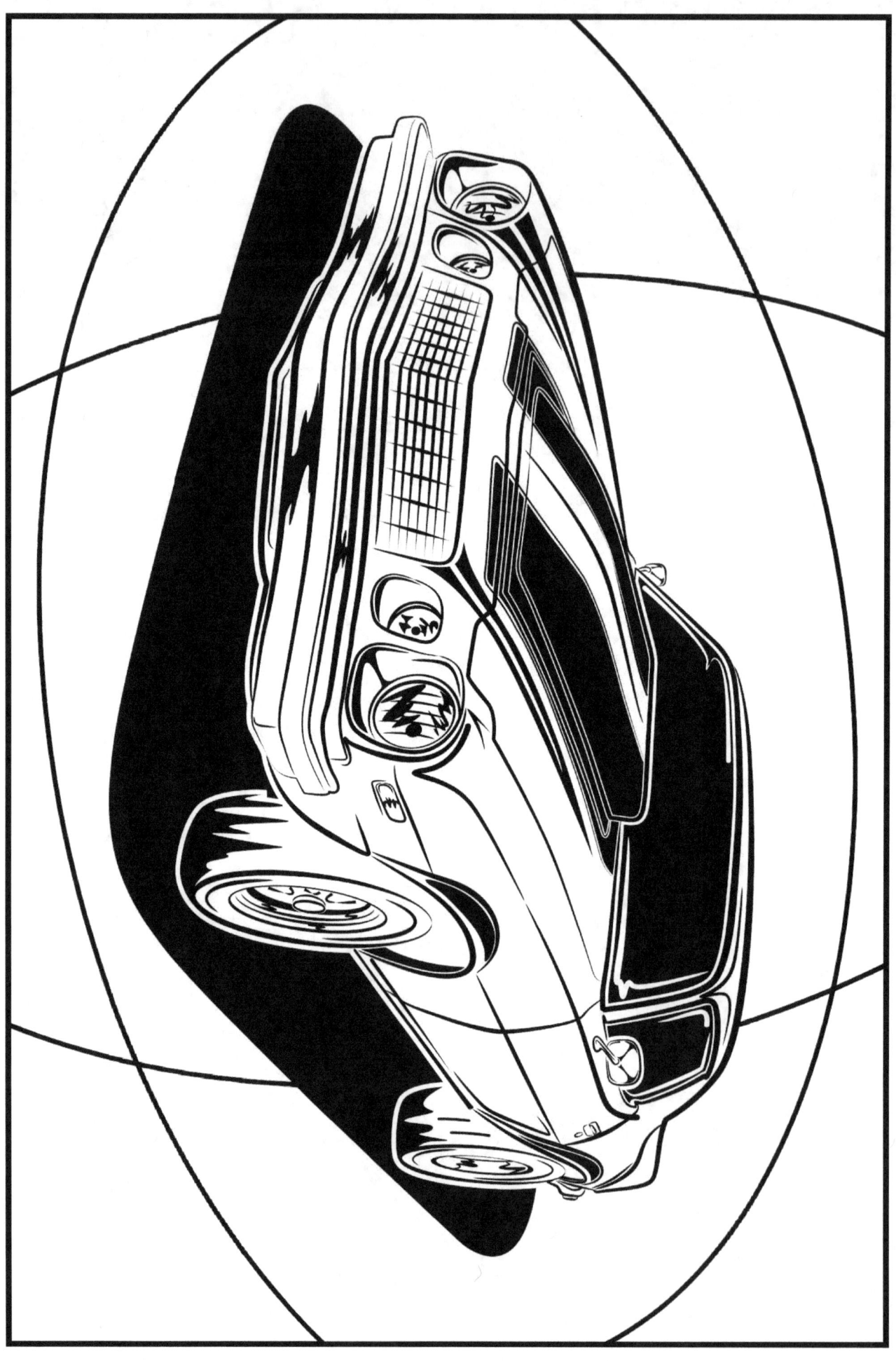

MUSCLE CARS

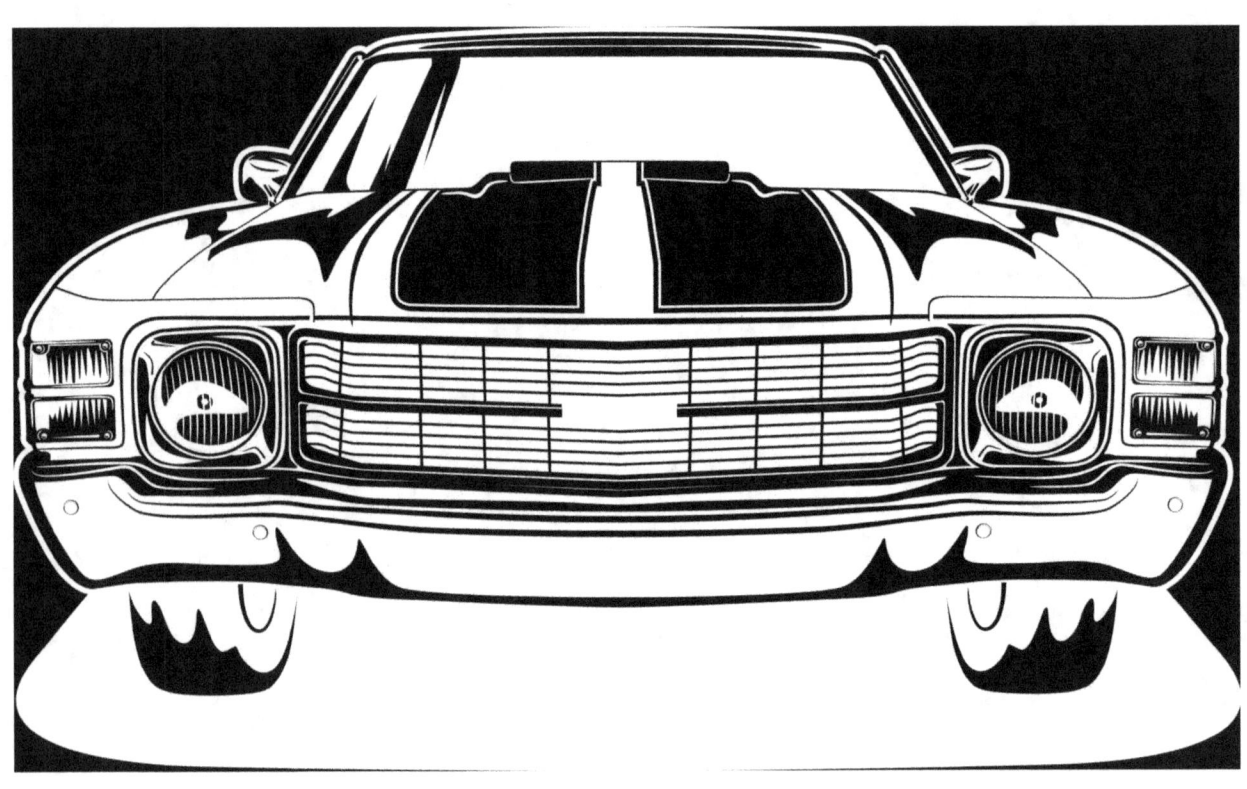

www.ingramcontent.com/pod-product-compliance
Lightning Source LLC
Chambersburg PA
CBHW062224220526
45471CB00009B/3340